RELATIONSHIPS

LOVE – MARRIAGE,

HATE – DIVORCE

&

KINKY SEX

"Trials, Tribulations and Fascinating
Stories of a Texas Divorce Lawyer"

Charles H. Robertson J.D.

Dedication

I have been working on this book for several years. It is Friday night, 8:33 P.M. on August 28, 2014 and I am sitting in front of my computer at home, while my wife, Ann, is cleaning up the kitchen. She has put up with me for fifty-four years. Our 50th wedding anniversary occurred on August 22, 2014. She and her sister, Dr. Sydney Bonnick have each proofread my work several times. I am grateful to both of them for their help.

This book is dedicated first to Ann and second to the wonderful clients I have had the pleasure of representing since September 15, 1969, the day I was sworn in as an attorney in Texas. Some of my clients have not been wonderful and they are specifically excluded from this dedication.

Preface

A number of my friends have told me that I am a good storyteller and that a lot of folks would enjoy my stories. I have been a divorce lawyer for forty-five years. In that time, I've found myself or my client in situations that were hysterically funny, or really uplifting, or just bizarre. About the time I think I have heard of every possible strange situation, here comes one even more unusual. My wife thinks that I just attract weird people. These stories are mostly true, with the names changed except in cases where my client is dead or a court has published an opinion about the case or I have permission to tell the story.

I have also written about my growing up in the Oak Cliff section of Dallas, my time in the Air Force and my experiences at Southern Methodist University School of Law. If you just want to read about the cases, the table of contents will allow you to do so. I hope you will read a little bit about my growing up and going to school. There are as many stories as you have time to read, so let me know if you enjoy them and I will write a second volume.

I hope that you enjoy the trip down memory lane as much as I have enjoyed reliving it.

If you would like to learn more about family law or about me, you can visit my website, *chrfamilylaw.com*
Charles H. Robertson
Doctor of Jurisprudence
SMU School of Law 1969

TABLE OF CONTENTS

INTRODUCTION

The Committee to Save Debra

The receptionist buzzed to tell me that there was a reporter from Washington, D. C., on the phone who wanted to talk about retaining me to help a little girl. My curiosity was piqued by the unusual nature of the request. When I got on the telephone, the person identified herself as the chairwoman of "The Committee to Save Debra." A group of television, radio and print journalists from the Washington D. C. area had formed the committee and contributed $3,000.00 to hire an attorney in Dallas, Texas, to save a six year old girl named Debra. I asked how in the world they had chosen me to help Debra. The lady explained that they had sought information from a number of sources to find an attorney who would protect Debra and raise hell with anyone who got in the way.

The story of Debra was interesting and disturbing. Six years before I received the call, a childless couple living in Baltimore, Maryland, had applied to adopt a child through Lutheran Social Services. A baby girl was located in Dallas, Texas who was eligible for adoption. It was explained to me that Dallas County Child Welfare had a policy of sending bi-racial children out of state for adoption. Debra's mother was African-American and her dad was Hispanic. I never was able to verify whether or not that was a policy, but Debra had been sent to Maryland. In Texas, adoption is a two-step process. First, the rights of the biological parents are terminated. Thereafter, the adoption can go forward after the child has been in the adoptive parent's home for six months and a social study has been completed, recommending the

3

adoption. Debra's adoptive parents had come to Dallas to pick her up and take her back to Baltimore. The social study was done and a favorable report was issued. Debra's adoptive parents were both excited and pleased with their beautiful baby girl.

Fast forward five years. Debra's mother and father were having big problems in their relationship. Debra's parents were later able to have a child of their own and had also adopted a male child. There were three children in the middle of a domestic disaster. Debra's mother filed for divorce. She was awarded the use of the family home and the primary care of the three children. Debra's father was bitter about what was happening and was becoming vindictive toward her mother. He checked the adoption records in Dallas and discovered that the Decree of Adoption had never been signed. Evidently, the clerk at Dallas County Child Welfare had put the file behind the drawer, instead of in the drawer, and the Decree of Adoption had never been finalized. At that time, Dallas County had a policy of not allowing adoptions by unmarried persons. Debra's father gleefully informed Dallas County that her mother was separated from him and would be single very soon. He thought there could be no better revenge than to have Debra taken away from her mother.

Unfortunately, Dallas County Child Welfare still had legal custody of Debra. They decided to stick to their policy of not allowing single parent adoptions and obtained a pick-up order for Debra. Lutheran Social Services, their agent in Baltimore, obtained an order to take Debra away from the only mother she had ever known and to return her to Dallas. The Washington media got wind of the story and it received substantial coverage in the newspapers and on television. There was a public outcry at the perceived injustice of the situation. I received the call from the chairwoman of the Committee to Save Debra as the court officers in Baltimore were trying to locate Debra in order to send her back to Dallas. "What in the world should we do?" she asked me, almost hysterically. My instructions were very simple and explicit:

1. Use some of the money you collected and put Debra, her mother and siblings on a flight to Dallas as fast as you can;
2. Call your reporter friends in Dallas and get them to pick up Debra and her family at the airport and give them a place to stay for a few days;
3. Give Debra's mom whatever is left of the money so that she can bring it to me.

My suggestions were followed and several print and television reporters picked up mom and the kids at the airport. They stayed at the homes of various media folks during the Texas proceedings. I received a call from a gentleman who identified himself as a producer for 60 Minutes on CBS. He told me that they would like to do a segment on Debra. My wife got all excited at the prospect of meeting Morley Safer or Mike Wallace.

My next move was unexpected by Child Welfare, which was represented by the District Attorney's office in Dallas. As the managing conservator of Debra, Dallas County Child Welfare had the right to give consent to or to veto an adoption request by Debra's mother, who thought the adoption had been granted five years before. They had made their position very clear, they did not intend to allow Debra to be adopted by a single person. The case I filed was for a change of managing conservatorship (custody for you non-Texans), because the burden was to show what was in the best interest of

Debra. Dallas County Child Welfare could not veto a change of custody. I stated that Dallas County Child Welfare had placed Debra with her mother and left her there for almost six years and should not be allowed to take the position that their placement was not in Debra's best interest. I also asked that the managing conservator be granted permission to approve Debra's adoption. If I prevailed in my custody case and Debra's mom was named managing conservator, she could consent to herself adopting Debra. The judge was a real jerk. He imposed a gag rule, stating that I could not talk to the press about the case. He did not want the public to find out what was going on in his court or learn of his rulings.

My ace in the hole was the assistant district attorney handling the case. Her name was Dee Miller. She was and is a person of integrity who really cared about the children in the cases she handled. We got a quick hearing. On the first day of the hearing, during a break, I stated to Dee Miller, "I cannot believe that you really think the position advocated by Dallas County Child Welfare is right. I am surprised that you and Mr. Wade, Henry Wade, the district attorney, would represent Dallas County Child Welfare and take the unreasonable position they are taking." Dee responded, "I'll talk to Mr. Wade."

The next day, the district attorney's office withdrew as counsel for Dallas County Child Welfare. The plan worked and Debra's mother was named her managing conservator. She now had the power to consent to Debra's being adopted. I recalled her as a witness and ask if she consented to Debra's being adopted by her. She granted herself permission to adopt Debra. The Judge was furious, I was pleased and

Debra was very happy!

It seemed like a fairy tale with a happy ending, but storm clouds were gathering in Baltimore. There had been a pick-up order in Baltimore to take Debra away from her mother and deliver her to Lutheran Social Services. When Debra, her mother and her two brothers returned to Baltimore, armed with her freshly signed Decree of Adoption, there was a contempt citation delivered to Debra's mother requiring her to come to court and face going to jail for not turning Debra over to Lutheran Social Services. The Baltimore judge, who was acting like he was the Dallas judge's twin brother, separated at birth, was furious that his pick-up order had not been successfully executed. Lutheran Social Services also wanted Debra's mother's hide.

Lutheran Social Services was functioning as the agent for Dallas County Child Welfare in Baltimore. Their authority to act was based solely on their employment as the agent for Dallas County, through Dallas County Child Welfare. The Dallas County District Attorney, Mr. Henry Wade had the authority to fire Lutheran Social Services. When I received a panic call reporting what was going on in Baltimore, I called Dee Miller. I pleaded with her to talk to Mr. Wade and get him to fire Lutheran Social Services. She called me with the bad news that she couldn't find Mr. Wade. I asked her to drive to the airport, buy a ticket on the first flight to Baltimore and to hope that she heard from Mr. Wade. Less than an hour later, she called back to tell me that she had been authorized to fly to Baltimore and to fire Lutheran Social Services in open court at the scheduled hearing. While Dee was in the air on the way to Baltimore, I called the Washington reporters and let them know what was happening. I was promised that a large contingent of the Washington/Baltimore press would be in the courtroom. Lutheran Social Services was fired, leaving no plaintiff in the case against Debra's mother. According to reports I received, the Judge was livid.

Dee Miller returned to Dallas to work as a juvenile district attorney. In a giant display of pettiness, the Baltimore judge filed a grievance against Dee in Dallas. It was dismissed without a hearing. I heard back from 60 Minutes that the story would have been much more interesting if I had failed in my efforts; so they would not be coming to Dallas. Evidently injustice gets better ratings than justice.

The rest of the story is that several years later, Dee Miller sought an appointment as a Judge of one of the two juvenile courts in Dallas County. The outgoing Judge, Pat McClung, who had been promoted to a position on the Dallas Court of Appeals, was familiar with Dee's work in his court as a district attorney. Dee was supported by Judge McClung, the organized bar and almost all of the attorneys who worked in the juvenile courts. It seemed like a match made in heaven. Character, integrity and diligence are qualities all attorneys hope for in the judges of the courts in which they practice.

Whoops!!! The appointments secretary for Texas Governor Dolph Briscoe wrote Dee's name opposite the 254th Family District Court, instead of the 304th Juvenile Court. Dee was the new judge of a divorce court, an area of law she had never practiced. It all worked out in the end. Dee Miller was the highest rated divorce judge in Dallas the year after she took the bench.

An embarrassing incident occurred regarding Judge Miller. I was in Austin, Texas at the State Bar headquarters grading family law specialization exams. The four members of the commission were all exhausted. It was four o'clock on Friday afternoon and we had been grading papers since about eight-thirty that morning. We had graded all but three or four of the exams and were pressing to make our flights back to our respective homes. I picked up one of the last papers which I could not read. I commented to the three other graders, "I refuse to grade this exam. It would give me a four Excedrin headache." To insure consistency in grading, each grader would grade the same one-fourth of each exam. The other commission members looked at the paper and agreed that we would not grade the exam. Two weeks later, we learned that we had refused to grade the specialization exam of Judge Dee Miller.

I called Judge Miller and offered to let Pat, her court reporter, transcribe the exam. After her exam was readable, it was graded. She passed with flying colors. I later appointed her to serve on the Family Law Examination Commission. She served until her doctor advised her to avoid air travel until after her baby was born. Dee Miller served long and well as a family law judge until she retired.

Social Security Cases

It is the summer of 1967. I have finished my first year of law school and am working at my first law-related job. I have secured a job as an intern at the Dallas Legal Services Project, a part of the Office of Economic Opportunity's War on Poverty. I was working under the supervision of a staff attorney, Maxine McConnell. She was an inspiration. Kind, caring, intelligent and hard-working is a tough combination to beat. It was my first experience with "common law marriage" issues. Our client was an elderly black lady in her eighties. While in her mid-thirties and early forties, she had been a cook in the White House while Calvin Coolidge and Herbert Hoover were serving their terms as president. She had returned to the Dallas area in the 1930's. She had been receiving Social Security survivor's benefits on the earnings record of her deceased husband. What brought her to our office was the receipt of a notice from the Social Security Administration that she would no longer receive benefits and she would have to repay over $28,000.00 in benefits which she had received in error. The letter went on to explain that the "real widow" was a lady in her early nineties, who lived in Waco, Texas. Maxine told me to find out what I could about the "husband" of the two ladies. It had shocked me to discover that White House staff workers had no benefits whatsoever. Roosevelt signed the Social Security Act in 1935. Before that there was no government program which helped retired or disabled government workers.

My investigation started with the goal of determining the marital history of the husband. I learned that he had come to Texas in the early thirties after having lived in Louisiana during his younger years. My search led me to the marriage and divorce records in Jefferson Parish, Louisiana. After several marriages and divorces in the early 1920's, the "husband" had remarried in 1928. He left Louisiana in the early 1930's and traveled to Waco, Texas, where he met the "Waco widow." Witnesses reported that his reputation for "loving and leaving" was well known in Louisiana. He had not filed for a divorce prior to leaving his 1928 wife, nor had she. He was still married to the lady in Louisiana when he started living with the lady in Waco. Living together, having sexual relations and holding out to be husband and wife to others was all it took in Texas to be married. The Waco widow thought she was married to him as did all of their friends and neighbors.

A basic principal of Texas law has always been that you could not enter into a valid marriage if you were already married to someone else. That principal I learned from this case would help me later. Our client had gone through a marriage ceremony with the "husband" after he moved to Dallas.

We challenged the determination of the Social Security Administration and lost in the first two stages of the proceedings. A suit was filed in Federal District Court, appealing the prior rulings. We lost again. The decision was made to file an appeal with the Federal Appeals Court in New Orleans. The records from Louisiana proved to be invaluable. We were able to show that there was never a divorce granted in either Louisiana or Texas to the husband and the wife he married in 1928. We were arguing that the Waco widow could not possibly be entitled to receive benefits if she had not ever been married to him. The "Eureka" moment occurred when I discovered that the Louisiana wife had died after the "husband" had left Waco and before he married our client in Dallas, Texas. The contractual impediment to entering into a valid marriage had been eliminated upon the death of the legal wife. Our client was the only legal widow. I had already returned to law school for my second year when the Federal Court of Appeals ruled in our favor. Our client, "Wife C" was entitled to receive survivor's benefits from her husband.

In the true spirit of compassion and understanding, the Social Security Administration demanded that "Wife B," the Waco widow, pay back all of the benefits she had received. I was surprised and pleased when I received a call from the "Waco widow" asking if there was any way I could help her against Social Security. She was in her nineties and living in a nursing home in Waco. I agreed to defend the claim against her. I found an obscure provision in the law which allowed the SSA to forgive the repayment of benefits under "extraordinary circumstances." I argued that there was no way for the "Waco widow" to have known that her "husband" did not have the legal right to enter into a common law marriage with her. I also suggested that a news conference might cause considerable negative publicity against the Social Security Administration under the circumstances.

I will never know why the Social Security Administration dropped their claim against my client. I was happy, the "Waco widow" was happy and my supervisor, Maxine McConnell, was both proud and happy.

Skip forward two years. It's 1969 and I have

13

graduated from law school, passed the bar examination and have started helping veterans who could not afford to pay an attorney. You will hear about the law school years later.

I discovered quickly the principal problem veterans were having with the Social Security Administration. Many of the veterans I helped would be declared to be 100% disabled by the Veterans Administration, only to be told by Social Security that they were not disabled at all. The definition of disability differed between the two agencies. I discovered that almost all of the initial applications filed for disability with Social Security were turned down. The process of trying to get disability benefits is anything but user friendly. I also discovered that an attorney helping social security disability applicants was eligible to receive 25% of the back benefits awarded to the claimant as attorney's fees. Depending on the facts, the claimant could receive benefits which would go back twelve months from the date of the application. I created a fee agreement which required no payment unless it could be taken from back benefits. The organization of the evidence, the artfully prepared application and the effective presentation of testimony were not commonplace at proceedings before the hearing examiners. People who handled their own cases seldom had success. The disability process had a number of levels. The application, the hearing, the appeals counsel and the suit in Federal Court were stages in the process. Almost all of the success came at the hearing stage. Marshalling the evidence and getting medical reports in evidence at the hearing were crucial. Lessons I had learned assisting the elderly lady while working for the Dallas Legal Services Project helped me do a better job for my clients. The Social Security Administration used the same experts regularly. A couple of their doctors would have claimed that a person in an "iron lung" was not disabled. One of the toughest cases to win was when you represented a client who did not look disabled at all.

One of the most rewarding cases I have handled in forty-five years of law practice was a social security disability case. The initial consultation was scheduled in the morning. The receptionist buzzed me to let me know the client had arrived. I got up, put on my coat and went out to the reception area to meet my prospective client. There were two people seated there. I did not know which person was my new client. I assumed that the woman was the client and that her husband had brought her to the office. I was about six feet, two inches tall, and weighed around 180. The lady was taller than me and probably fifty pounds heavier. Her husband was at least 6'6" and probably weighed 300. He was a massive man with very muscular arms. He looked like he could pick up the rear end of my Chevy.

D.J. Brown and his wife, Daisy, followed me back to my office. I asked how I could help them. Daisy answered that D.J. had been turned down for Social Security disability benefits. She explained that he had congestive heart failure and had suffered several heart attacks. D.J. had been a construction worker who had made good money until he started having heart trouble. The problem was that he looked like he could be playing defensive tackle for the Dallas Cowboys. I reviewed the application which had been filed and immediately saw that mistakes had been made which had probably caused the request not to be seriously considered. I set forth a plan of action, which included getting D.J. to a doctor who could give us a good report about the seriousness of his condition. No medical information had been included with the application for benefits. The more I talked to Daisy, the more I liked her. She and D.J., who spoke precious few words during the almost two hour consultation, had four children. The three daughters were all in school, two in college and one a senior in high school. They lived close to the area of Dallas where I grew up. Their son, Billy, was a sophomore in high school. Daisy was working two, eight hour a day jobs to keep the family afloat. She worked sixteen hours on many days in the laundries of two Dallas hospitals. From that day until the last time I talked to Daisy, she called me "Lawyer Robeson." We agreed that she would be the contact person to keep D.J. from getting upset and worried.

I was able to arrange for D.J. to see an excellent cardiologist. As I suspected, D.J. was in really bad shape. The doctor was afraid that another heart attack would be D.J.'s last. We planned our hearing presentation carefully. It was rare for a medical witness to appear in person at a hearing, but very effective. D.J.'s employer, Daisy and the two older girls were extremely well spoken. The doctor had agreed to participate at the hearing. Several weeks before the hearing I received a call from Daisy.

"Lawyer Robeson, I need some emotional support. I have to whip Billy every morning to make him go to school. Billy is saying that he is going to quit school and get a job to help me." I asked, "How old is Billy?" "He is sixteen," she responded. "How tall is Billy and how much does he weigh?" "He is 6'4" and weighs 250 and it is all I can do to whip him and make him go to school." "Will you have Billy call me?" I asked. When he called, I explained how important it was to his mother for him to stay in school, graduate and go to college. I told him that we should hear soon about the decision and we could talk more if the decision was not favorable. Billy agreed to stay in school for the time being.

The hearing had gone extremely well and I was waiting at the front desk every day at mail delivery time. The decision finally arrived! D.J. was found to be disabled, was awarded back benefits of $12,000.00 and monthly payments including benefits for the children of $1,200 per month. I rushed back to my office to call Daisy. I found her at the laundry of her second job. I told her the decision and didn't have to wait for a response.

"Praise the Lord, thank you Jesus and you, Lawyer Robeson." She repeated the thanks several times and then stated, "Lawyer Robeson, I have a right personal question to ask you. Have you ever been kissed by a black woman?" "No" I responded. "Well you gonna be."

The check for the back benefits had arrived with the decision letter. Daisy and D.J. were coming to the office to pick up the check. I expected that I was going to get kissed, whether I wanted to or not. They came into my office for a brief visit. It was the only time I ever saw D.J. smile. I handed the check and Daisy reached across and took it out of my hand. I stood up to show them out, thinking I might not be kissed after all. Daisy looked at me, stepped forward and gave me a big hug and a kiss on the cheek. She stepped back, wiggled and said, "One's just not enough" stepped forward and gave another hug and a kiss on the other cheek.

Daisy may well be my favorite all time client. The girls all graduated from college as did Billy. The last time I talked to Daisy, she told me that Billy and one of his sisters were school teachers. D.J. died four or five years after he started receiving benefits.

Growing Up In Oak Cliff

I grew up in a part of Dallas called Oak Cliff. It was a part of town which had fought not to be a part of the bigger city. I lived in a federal housing project called Dallas Park. It was developed during World War II to house people who worked in the aircraft industry principally located in Grand Prairie, Texas, just west of Dallas. Oak Cliff was considered a less desirable part of Dallas, located west of the Trinity River. My father had worked since he was a teenager as a "printer's devil" and then as a linotype operator at the Dallas Morning News. He took a leave of absence when World War II started and helped organize a program to teach workers how to use machinery which produced parts needed to manufacture airplanes at North American Aviation. I was born in Dallas at Baylor Hospital in the Florence Nightingale maternity wing just twelve days after the Japanese bombed Pearl Harbor. Because my dad had helped start the cross-training program to help in the war effort, we were offered a house in Dallas Park. We lived on Barksdale Court in the far western part of Dallas. All of the streets were named after Air Force Bases. Our house was on the corner of Randolph and Barksdale. Lakehurst, Orlando, Chanute and Pensacola were some of the other streets. My earliest memories revolve around a bird dog that used to take my half of an orange away from me. My mother would cut an orange in half and give me and my older brother equal parts of the orange. She would let us go outside the house to eat the orange in order to create less of a mess in the house. Our neighbor, Fred Adcock, had a reddish-brown and white bird dog that was very friendly and gentle. My problem was that the dog loved oranges. She would come up to me and take the orange out of my hand with her mouth and run away to polish off the orange. The next vivid memory I have is when I was playing in the sand box beside the house. Mom had received a call that a rabid collie was loose in the neighborhood. She rushed outside to bring me into the house. The dog, frothing at the mouth, was running toward me when she reached the sandbox. She grabbed me and held me above her head as the dog approached. The dog bit her on both legs. Neighbors chased the dog away, but only after he had hurt Mom pretty badly. I was unscathed. After Mom was stitched up, there was nothing to do until the report came back from the laboratory at Texas A&M about whether the dog had hydrophobia. The news was bad, which meant that Mom had to go through a long series of shots into her stomach. I was deathly afraid of all dogs until I was in my forties.

It was an interesting neighborhood. There were lots of kids with whom I could play. There was a community center with meeting rooms and recreation facilities. There were planned activities for children in the summer. Until I was about eight years old, Mrs. Caulfield and her mother took care of me as one of the younger children. I think I was eight and about to start the third grade when I was allowed to join the big kids program. The director of the summer program for the older kids was Frank Guzick. He was a coach at Dallas Adamson High School during the school term. He had been a small college All-American football player at Texas Tech. He later attended the United States Coast Guard Academy. He was a tall, athletic man who was always in control of everything around him. I learned later that he was the first Jewish person to be an assistant principal in the Dallas Independent School District. I knew him as my next door neighbor who ran the recreation program during the summer. He was also the greatest story teller I have ever listened to in person. There were enough boys for three baseball teams. Six games were played each week. One day per week there was a double-header. The baseball games started early in the morning during the summer to escape the Texas heat. As soon as the game was concluded, we would all rush to the Coke machine. Cokes in hand, we would head to the shade of the north side of the building. Mr. Guzick would sit in a folding wooden chair with at least twenty boys sitting around him, eager to hear the day's story. Some of the stories could be concluded at one sitting, but more often it would take three, four or even five days to finalize the spellbinding tales. It was like the serials you went to see on Saturdays at the neighborhood Cockrell Hill Theater. Flash Gordon, Lash Larue or Zorro were no better than Guzick's daily stories. I learned how to play baseball, Ping-Pong, horseshoes and basketball under the tutelage of the man we affectionately called "The Guze." Frank Guzick was a tremendous influence in my formative years and was an excellent role model. He went from being a coach at Adamson High School, to being the assistant Principal at Sunset High School, where I attended. He left Sunset to be the principal at Rylie Junior High School. From there, Frank Guzick became the principal of Skyline High School, the largest high school in the United States. He was the principal at Skyline until he retired. He was a firm disciplinarian. Frank Guzick Elementary School is now one of the newer elementary schools in Dallas. Hundreds of

21

former students attended his funeral.

I went to school to play sports. My best sport was basketball. I made the All-City team in Dallas my senior year. I was one of the few varsity athletes who participated in the special academic program. It was almost like a private school. There were sixteen girls and five guys in my English class. The math and science classes were dominated by boys. One of the smartest things I did in high school was to cajole Barry Schwarz, probably the smartest person in our class, to be my chemistry lab partner. We were sailing right along until he got chicken pox the last week of the semester. Our teacher, Mr. Cecil Jerden, based the last six weeks grade heavily on your success in finding the "unknowns" in a solution of liquid. With Barry there, it would have been a "piece of cake." Most of the teams were given two or three unknowns in the solution. I correctly suspected that our solution was really loaded in an attempt to challenge the class genius, who just happened to be at home with the chicken pox. Fortunately, I had already experienced chicken pox. I worked diligently each day and hurried over to Barry's house after school to report my progress. Guided by my spotted partner, I found five different compounds in the unknown solution. Barry came back to school the day our teacher announced our results. Five out of six got us an A. I still think Mr. Jerden was really jerking us around by giving us sodium chloride and potassium chloride in our solution. The only way to differentiate the two compounds is with a flame test, during which sodium chloride creates a more yellow color while potassium chloride has more of an orange hue.

I loved school and was the perpetrator of a number pranks during my years at Sunset. I was the vice-president of the student body my senior year. The president presided at the assemblies of the student body before football games and other sporting events. I am positive that the principal, Mr. H.S. Griffin, prayed before each assembly that Marshall Martin, the president of the student body, would not be sick and unable to preside at the assemblies.

I didn't realize Oak Cliff was not the best part of town until after I went to Southern Methodist University, which was in an enclave called the Park Cities. The Park Cities included Highland Park and University Park and were totally surrounded by north Dallas.

SMU provided real culture shock. I had never seen so many rich kids in my life. Sunset's attendance zone had a small area of really affluent families living in Kessler Park, but was principally either middle class or lower middle class. I didn't realize that where I lived was considered to be a "lower class" place. I learned to "Persevere in the Face of Adversity."

Life in the Air Force

I was able to go to law school on vocational rehabilitation while on the Temporary Deferred Retired List of the United States Air Force. How I got on the list was a result of what transpired while on active duty in the Air Force. I had a series of athletic injuries before entering the service, but none which kept me from participating in physical training or sports. While I was stationed at Eglin Air Force Base in the Florida Panhandle, I injured my left knee on two occasions.

It was our first wedding anniversary. I was hitting practice golf balls in the back yard of our home in Fort Walton Beach while Ann got ready for our big dinner date. After a mighty swing at a practice ball, my left knee locked and I fell to the sandy ground. I was about thirty feet from the back door. I tried to stand, but failed several times. I called for Ann, who was in the house, but I received no response. Crawling to the back door seemed to be my only choice. After considerable effort, I managed to get close enough to the door to bang on it with the golf club I had been using to hit the practice shots. Ann came to the back door wearing one of those inflatable caps which connected to a hair dryer. After I explained what had happened, she helped me get to the bedroom. I was able to get my right leg onto the bed along with most of my body. I was lying on my stomach. I asked her if she could help me get my left leg, the one I could not bend, up on the bed. Now Ann is left-handed and has always confused right and left. She thought I was asking for help in getting my right leg, which was not hurt, up on the bed. After saying she would, she grabbed my left foot and threw the leg up on the bed. I screamed in pain as cracking and popping sounds emanated from the injured knee which was now on the bed and was no longer in a locked position. I was sure that the cartilage was torn and part of it got into the joint and kept the knee from bending. But my wife had "fixed" my knee, at least for the time being. Ann went to get a bottle of wine and a pizza for our anniversary dinner.

A few weeks later, I was playing softball with some Air Force buddies. I was the pitcher when a guy bunted down the third-base line. I fielded the ball and wheeled to throw to first. The toe cleats on my left shoe caught in the grass. My body weight rotated on top of my left knee. My chest was facing first base; my left foot still pointed to third. This time there was no quick fix. I was admitted to the base hospital for a thorough evaluation of my left knee. The report was not good. I had torn my posterior and anterior cruciate ligaments and my lateral co-lateral ligament. The cartilage was also torn. Reconstructive surgery was scheduled to try and repair the ligaments. Surgical repair of torn ligaments was not nearly as sophisticated as it is today. After a stay in the hospital and a long period in a cast, the knee was reexamined and found to be just as unstable as before the surgery. The cartilage that had been removed had thirteen separate tears. I was sent to the chief orthopedist for the region at Keesler Air Force Base in Mississippi for further evaluation. After a lengthy exam he asked me, "Who did this to you, son?" I told him the doctor's name and he responded, "That's impossible, he is not a surgeon."

I was confused and angry. I found out later that my doctor really wanted to be a surgeon and decided to practice on me. I didn't know if my knee would affect my service commitment or whether I would ever be able to get around normally. I was "bone on bone" in my left knee with only one of the four ligaments you need to have a stable knee joint. The medial ligament on the right side of my left knee was the only one left intact. The first thing I did was to buy the best knee brace I could find, with hinged steel supports on each side of the knee.

I was a part of 729th Communications and Control Squadron, which was a part of the Tactical Air Command or TAC. The entire squadron had been killed in the Korean conflict and was re-formed when Viet Nam started to heat up. I was a weapons controller. The Army called their personnel who did the same job forward air controllers. The Army operated out of light aircraft and the Air Force operated out of a module in the cargo part of a two and one-half ton truck. The basic job of either the Army or Air Force was to control aircraft and to direct them to targets. The Air Force controllers also had the responsibility of selecting which method of attack and which weapon to use in combat with enemy aircraft. The Army thought they could do a superior job of controlling the aircraft once they reached the target area. The Air Force thought that it could do a superior job. This dispute gave rise to several field exercises where the two branches competed. After three exercises, the results were dead even.

One of the exercises resulted in the only commendation medal I received during my time in the service. The exercise was conducted on the border of Arkansas and Missouri. Our camp was set up under the direction of a captain we all called "Blinky." The latrines were constructed with four by eight foot pieces of plywood. A circle saw was used to cut holes in the plywood for the user to sit over. The first day they were in use, the Colonel got a three inch splinter in his backside. He was furious. He screamed at Blinky for several minutes. Now Blinky was not the sharpest knife in the drawer and was scared that he would not make the rank of major, which would allow him to stay in the service for twenty years and be eligible for retirement. I told the distraught captain that if he would give me a driver and a jeep, I would solve the problem. The driver appeared and we took off to the closest town. I ask a local for directions to the nearest junk yard. After locating the junk yard, I bought the toilet seat and lid combination off of four cracked toilets. We hurried back to camp to install the seats and lids over the holes made by the circle saw. The Colonel was pleased, the captain was ecstatic and I had earned my one and only commendation medal while serving in the United States Air Force.

The rumors had started flying that many members of the squadron were going to receive orders to go to Viet Nam. I called a friend at TAC headquarters at Langley AFB, Virginia, to make what I thought was a very logical inquiry.

"Is there any assignment in the world for someone with my Air Force Specialty Code (AFSC) for which no one has ever volunteered?"

"Why in the world would you want to know?" he responded. "Just tell me if such a place exists," I answered. To his surprise, there were two such places, both north of the Arctic Circle. My AFSC included being a radar officer who could perform an air defense function by watching Russia. I put in volunteer statements for both locations immediately. Several days later, I received word that I was to report to the base psychiatrist. I reported to the base hospital and was shown in to see the psychiatrist. He looked at me and asked, "Son, what are you up to?" I explained that our entire original squadron had been killed in the Korean conflict and that more than fifty percent of the officers who had gone to Viet Nam had been killed. I told him that I would rather take a chance of my ass being frozen off than being shot off. He smiled broadly and said, "There's nothing wrong with you, good luck."

Alaska, here I come. All I had to do was pass the remote physical and I would be in the frozen north for a year. After a remote tour, I could choose an accompanied tour in Europe to finish my commitment to the Air Force. The down side was that I would be gone for a year. The upside was that my wife, Ann, and I could spend two years in Europe. The appointment for the physical was set and I went to the hospital the next week. To my great surprise, I discovered when I checked in that the doctor who had operated on my knee was scheduled to give me the physical. There was nothing said about my knee except that the doctor said he was sorry that they had not been able to fix the problems. After a very thorough physical, I went into the doctor's office to discuss the results. He told me that I had not passed the physical. He explained that I had arthritis in both knees from playing sports for years and that the cold weather would make it a lot worse.

Our squadron was on a four hour alert status to be sent anywhere to set up a mobile air traffic control facility. If you ever flunked a physical, you would be discharged from the service. I was going to be out of the Air Force quickly. The base counselor explained to me that I might be eligible to be placed on the Temporary Deferred Retired List and have an option to attend graduate school under a vocational rehabilitation program, if I could pass the required entrance exams. I signed up to take the Law School Aptitude Test. I had already taken the Graduate Records Exam to get into graduate school. I also applied for admission and for a scholarship to SMU Law School in Dallas, my home town.

Philosophy

My philosophy of life and how people should be treated and how law should be practiced is a product of many components. Contributions have been made by people who taught me what should be done and people who have taught me what should not be done. My mother, who died on August 11, 2011 at age 97, taught me the most about what should be done. She also taught me a good bit about what should not be done. I will give you examples of both as I go on with this chapter. My mother's mother served as a great example of what should be done. Grandmother was a great teacher. Her work ethic and her attitude about other people were inspiring. I had some great teachers in school, from grade school through law school and later as a practicing lawyer. Coaches, doctors, neighbors, high school classmates and golf buddies have all taught me about what is important. I am very hesitant to name most of the people who have been examples of what not to do.

I take great pleasure in naming the people who have been examples of how I believe we should treat each other. My greatest and best teacher has been my wife, Ann. We have been married since August 22, 1964. She is a great example of how hard work and responsibility pay off. She made 37 A's and 3 B's in four years of college at SMU. She was elected to Mortar Board and Phi Beta Kappa. If there is one correct answer to a problem, don't bet against her or you will lose. The other teachers who have taught me invaluable lessons are Fluffy, Andy, Rufus and Quincy, our dogs. The cats will not be named because they have taught me what I shouldn't do. One exception would be my current tomcat, Amos, who thinks he is a dog.

My mother, Dorris Harriet Giltner Robertson was born July 25, 1914. She was six feet tall when she was twelve years old. She was a perfect mesomorph. Her bone and muscle structure would have been the envy of any athlete. I could not beat her arm wrestling until I was a junior in high school. She was tough, but fair. Any time I was to be disciplined, I had to sit down in a chair while mom was standing. She looked like a giant. I did not ever challenge her authority, even after I was taller and stronger. Mom had one rule that I think did more to help me learn how to think outside of the box than all the years of my formal education. The rule was simple: You have no right to complain about anything unless you have a proposed solution. From time to time I would complain and she would tell me to sit down in a chair while she stood over me during our discussion.

For a long period of time when I was in grade school, we did not have a car. Mom and Dad both worked and rode the bus to and from work. As a result of having to ride the bus home, it was not uncommon for us to eat supper about 7:00 p.m. or a little later. During the summer before the sixth grade, I complained about having to eat so late. She sat me down and asked me for a solution. I thought for a minute and then said, "Teach me how to cook." I became a good cook and would often have supper ready when Mom and Dad got home. Her rule not only taught me to think, it also taught me to be responsible. I remember her asking me if I had done my homework. I replied that her question was offensive. I proposed that she never ask me that again until after I made my first B on my report card. She never asked me again. She explained that rules had to be made because people were not responsible. She suggested that real freedom could only exist if perfect responsibility existed at the same time. She never got to go to college, but she was very intelligent. She was a voracious reader until her death.

I found out during my senior year in high school that if Mom could get a job at SMU, I could go to school on a faculty and staff scholarship. She was working as a cashier at a Skillern's drug store at the time. I got her an employment application from SMU and she prepared a resume. She applied for four different jobs and got job offers for each. She accepted the position as the cashier at the student union book store. Mom and I commuted to SMU from Oak Cliff for several years. She really liked having contact with many of the students, principally from the undergraduate schools. In addition to teaching me how to cook, she taught me how to sew, how to wallpaper and how to paint. I remember how disappointed I was in high school when the school refused to allow me to take home economics. The principal was convinced I wanted to take the course in order to be the only boy in a class of young ladies. I cannot say that the idea had not crossed my mind.

I always went to summer school early in the morning before I went to work at my summer jobs. The summer school teachers were always thrilled to have a few good students in the class with all of the kids who were there because they had failed the first time they took the course. The A's almost fell out of the sky. I could have graduated early except for the fact that my main interest in going to school was to play sports.

I had a brother who was one year older than me. We went to Cockrell Hill Elementary School until the new elementary school, L.O. Donald, could be completed. Cockrell Hill Elementary was too small for the number of students and some of classes were taught in the Cockrell Hill Baptist Church which was next door. L.O. Donald opened in time for me to start the second grade. My teacher, Mrs. Hale, was really good. Her daughter, Hazael, has been a life-long friend of mine. Our principal was Miss Eugenia Becker, who was "out to lunch" most of the time. I will never forget her having spanked me because she heard I had, "stolen second base."

My one good memory of Miss Becker relates to an incident involving the best school teacher I ever had, bar none. Miss Ulyssa Jo Perkins was my third grade teacher. She made her students want to learn. She was a true inspiration. Her greatest gift was to create in her students the joy of learning. Miss Perkins taught me more about spelling, grammar and word usage than any high school or college teacher. She talked me into sending one of my first poems to the "Weekly Reader" for possible publication. "Australian Animals" was published and I have been writing poems ever since. We all knew she loved us and we felt the same way about her.

Toward the end of my third grade year, Miss Perkins fell and broke her leg while square dancing. After several weeks at home, she returned to our class. She was our home room teacher, which meant that she taught us everything except music, art and physical education. Some of us heard a rumor that the third grade classrooms would be moved to the second floor of the school building. That would mean that Miss Perkins would have to climb the stairs. I suggested that our class protest the proposed move which would be hard on our teacher. The plan was for us all to get to school early one morning and go into Miss Perkins' classroom. Her room was directly across the hall from the principal's office. The school office had a long counter. At the left end of the counter was a door to the principal's office. That office had a door that lead directly to the hall in front of Miss Perkins classroom. The door to the hall did not open from the hall; it opened only from inside the office. My plan was to sneak into the office and crawl across the floor in front of the counter so the ladies behind the counter could not see me and I could get into the principal's office. Once inside the principal's office, I would open the door to the hall and signal for my classmates to join me. The plan worked flawlessly. Once inside the office, we all sat down on the floor around the principal's desk and locked our arms. All we had to do now was to wait for Miss Becker to come into her office. When she appeared, we would state our demand and let her know that we were prepared to sit around the desk until our demand was met. Our demand was simple, "Miss Perkins will not have to move her classroom off of the ground floor." After just a few minutes, Miss Becker appeared through the office door. "What in the world are you doing here?" , she asked. The plan was for several people to speak out so not just one would shoulder the blame. We are here to demand that Miss Perkins classroom stay on the ground floor next year. "Why might that be," she asked. We believe that Miss Perkins will not be able to climb the stairs because of her leg and might have to retire. If that happened, you would lose your best teacher and it would deprive others of the wonderful year we have had in her class. Miss Becker looked puzzled. "I'll be back," she said.

Miss Becker returned and to our great amazement said, "If you all care that much about your teacher, she will not have to go to the second floor and she will be your fourth grade teacher." In a much more authoritarian tone, Miss Becker said, "Now get up and get to class." My first act of civil disobedience had worked. Not only that, I was going to get to have the world's best teacher for another whole year. My other years in grade school were not as good as those two great years with Miss Perkins.

In the seventh grade I had another great teacher. Mrs. Janice Romanio was really special. She was a world champion female airplane racer. We had a six week long period during which we studied the history of aviation. From Dadelus and Iccarus to the Montgolfiers to the Wright brothers and beyond, Mrs. Ramanio made the history of aviation come alive. Toward the end of the period, I ask if I could try to talk an airline into taking us for a ride. "It's worth a try" she told me. I got the feeling that she didn't think there was much of a chance that I would succeed. To everyone's surprise and excitement, Braniff Airlines agreed. Our class went to Love Field in Dallas where we boarded a DC-4, took off, flew around north Texas and landed back at Love Field. My picture was in the paper with the captain and a flight attendant.

During the sixth and seventh grades, I got really fat. I had always been skinny until I broke my left wrist three times in a row. My sport activities were really restricted, but I kept eating as usual. By the end of the seventh grade I was five feet, six inches tall and weighed almost 180. I played guard on the football team in the eighth grade and didn't get to play much in basketball, which was always my favorite sport. I will never forget how embarrassed I was at a party where they were playing "Spin the Bottle." A really cute blond girl named Cathy spun the bottle and it came to rest pointing at me. She reached out for the bottle to spin again and said," I don't kiss fat boys." My first experience with dieting started the next day.

I listened to radio station KMOX out of St. Louis. It was the only station my radio could bring in which broadcast professional basketball. The St. Louis Hawks had a great team. Bob Petit, Clyde Lovellette, Cliff Hagen and Slater Martin were my favorites. If you haven't figured it out by now, let me tell you that I have a weird memory. I still remember my grade school friends' phone numbers. None of the numbers or exchanges exist today. There is no correlation between memory and intelligence, but having a great memory pays off in funny ways. Cliff Hagen was a 6'4" guy from Kentucky who led the NBA in rebounding. I desperately wanted to increase my jumping ability and my improve rebounding. I wrote Cliff Hagen a letter asking for suggestions. To my delight he answered my letter and gave me the basics of a program which I followed through high school.

I had bet my brother that I would earn a school letter on a ninth grade team while I was in the eighth grade. Football and basketball had passed and I had not lettered. Baseball, track and tennis were the only chances I had left. I was a catcher in baseball, and would have been playing behind two of the best catchers in my age group in the city. Track offered little opportunity for a short fat kid. I decided to go out for the tennis team. I signed up on Friday to try out for the team and told the coach that I had played a lot in the park during the previous summer.

I had never played tennis in my life and did not know the rules or the terminology of the game. Tryouts were to begin on Monday afternoon. First thing Saturday morning I went to the downtown Dallas Public Library. I checked out three books on tennis and headed off to a pawn shop. I paid $3.00 for my first racket and bought a can of three tennis balls from Sears. While on the bus to get back home I was reading about forehands, backhands, service and the rules. I spent the rest of the day devouring the books on how to play tennis. After church on Sunday and a quick lunch, I went to the closest park that had a tennis court with a backboard so I could try to learn how to hit the ball. My advantage was that very few good athletes played tennis during that era. I knew that I would have more natural athletic ability than any of the boys trying out for the team. My plan worked. I played either number one or two on the boys' team all season. We played well enough to win the doubles championship for our zone. I won the bet and became a tennis player that spring of 1954. As a matter of fact, I was playing tennis at Kiest Park in Oak Cliff when a very destructive tornado passed several hundred feet east of the courts and tore the roofs off of many houses.

I am not sure why or how it happened, but when I reported for football practice in the fall of the ninth grade, I had grown six inches and lost forty pounds since the end of the previous football season. Instead of being the short fat kid the coaches had playing guard the year before, I was a tall skinny kid. The first day of practice, Coach Reeves, who was the head coach, approached me and said, "Are you new to the school? I don't think I've met you." I reminded him who I was and that I had played well enough in the eighth grade to get to suit up for some ninth grade games. He said, "I cannot believe how much you have grown. We need to get some more weight on you as soon as possible." I had always fancied myself as a quarterback or a receiver. I wasn't interested in playing offensive line, blocking for a tailback weighing 175 who could run like a deer. When I told Coach Reeves I wanted to be a receiver, he did not respond positively.

Later that day, the basketball coach saw me dunking a dodge ball in the gym. I had worked hard every day since Cliff Hagen had sent me his suggestions for how I could become a better jumper and rebounder. The year before, I had not been able to touch the bottom of the net, which was about sixteen inches below the ten foot high rim. He pulled me aside and told me that I shouldn't be wasting my time playing football. My football career ended that afternoon. I was then and am still very near sighted. Without my glasses, which I had been wearing since the third grade, I couldn't have seen the football well enough to catch it, let alone find the receivers on my team if I had tried to play quarterback. Basketball would be my primary sport through high school. I made friends on the basketball team I still see regularly.

My high school class was over 500 members. I was the vice-president of the student body of over 1600 students. I receive between 20 and 30 emails a day from classmates who graduated in 1960. Every spring, between 20 and 26 of the guys from my high school class go to a ranch in west Texas near Abilene and spend five days together. We are all now seventy or older. We play golf and poker, pitch horseshoes, fish, tell lies, drink and eat gourmet food. I have always been very active in the planning of our high school reunions. Continued contact with friends is one of my great pleasures in life. My grandmother had told me before I started the first grade that if you are a friend to others, you will always have more friends than you can count.

My second group of great friends is comprised of my golf buddies. Most of them play at Royal Oaks Country Club in Dallas. Another group of golf buddies were in my high school class at Sunset High School. I try to play two to three times per week. I am a very mediocre golfer.

Also good friends are the lawyers I have known since law school at Southern Methodist University and the ones I have worked with and against for the past forty-five years. I have met thousands of good lawyers through the family law sections of the State Bar of Texas, the American Bar Association and the American Academy of Matrimonial Lawyers. Friends are more important than gold.

CASES

YOUNG V. YOUNG 609 S.W.2d 758, Texas Supreme Court

When Laura Young came to see me, she told me she had tried to work with three previous attorneys with no success. She did not know where her husband was living. It had been several years since she had seen or heard from him. They had previously lived in Grand Prairie, Texas. Her husband worked for Ling Temco Vaught, LTV, a defense contractor. The Young's had a son and a daughter. Mr. Young was told he was being transferred from the plant in Texas to the Kentron division in Florida. For several years, the family lived in Florida while Mr. Young worked for Kentron. He told Laura that he had decided to retire. He suggested she move the children and Mr. Young's mother back to their Texas home, which had been rented while they were in Florida. One reason he gave for the family's moving back to Texas was for the children to start school in the fall. Laura acceded to his wishes and returned to Grand Prairie with the son, daughter and Mr. Young's mother. Mr. Young said he would return during the fall to be with his family.

It had been almost three years since Laura had moved back to Texas and she had not seen or heard from her husband. Things had changed at home. Her son, who had been attending Texas A&M, had been diagnosed with multiple sclerosis. Mr. Young's mother was having severe kidney problems and could not control her bladder. Her daughter was a pregnant and unmarried teenager. Not only had Mr. Young not called or come by, he had not provided any financial support. Laura was trying to work two jobs and was receiving food stamps and other state aid.

Laura insisted that she would not be a charity case. She said that if I decided to help her, she would make monthly payments. She paid me five dollars a month for years. I finally found Mr. Young living in a wealthy district in Houston with a young lady who had worked with him in Florida. Surprisingly, she and Mr. Young were representing themselves to be married. I was able to find records of a divorce in Mexico, which showed that Mr. and Mrs. Young had received an agreed divorce in Mexico several years earlier. Laura knew nothing of the purported divorce and her signature on the documents had been forged. Mr. Young had actually gone through a marriage to his new lady friend. I never found out if the new "Mrs. Young" was the woman who impersonated Laura and forged her name on the divorce documents in Mexico.

The divorce case was filed in Dallas County, Texas. After several years and many heartaches and unreasonable burdens on Laura, Mr. Young had to face the music. The judge of the court where the case was filed had gone to college, seminary and then law school. He had a soft heart and could become very protective of people who had been mistreated. During the trial, he became emotional on several occasions and called short recesses. His decision was precedent setting. I had asked him to consider the fault of Mr. Young in the breakup of the marriage and the needs of the adult disabled son in his division of the property. Those two criteria had never been used as a justification for a disproportionate division of the parties' property. The judge awarded ninety-eight percent (98%) of the property to Laura Young. He explained that he would have awarded all of the property to her, but for the fact that two percent (2%) was in the girlfriend's name. He awarded a ten thousand dollar ($10,000.00) fee to me even though I had not requested it nor had I put on any evidence about the value of the time I had spent.

The attorney for Mr. Young told me he intended to appeal. He filed the appeal and we responded. We waited for the decision. It is not uncommon to have to wait six months or more to receive the decision from the Court of Appeals. I was surprised and angry when the Dallas Court of Appeals in a decision written by Justice Spencer Carver reversed the trial court decision and remanded the case back to the lower court for a new trial. Justice Carver stated that the trial court judge should not have to listen to "every nag, bicker and pout" of a disgruntled wife. He went on to say that fault in the breakup of the marriage and the needs of an adult disabled child could not be a basis for a disproportionate division of the property. I called Justice Carver and asked him why nothing had been said about the attorney's fee award. He said not to worry, that would be taken care of upon remand. I told him that I intended to file a writ, asking the Texas Supreme Court to review the Appeals Court decision. He smugly said, "Go ahead and file it. You don't have a snowball's chance in Hell of it being granted."

I really didn't need his condescending, patronizing statement to get me cranked up about filing the writ to the Texas Supreme Court. I did start thinking about how I could use his words against him at some time in the future. The likelihood of getting the Texas Supreme Court to hear the case was not good. The odds of the court granting the writ so that the case could be presented were about one in a thousand. The

Supreme Court had historically shown little interest in family law questions. If two courts of appeals had ruled in a contradictory fashion on the same issue, the court might hear the question to clarify the law. The other reason for the court to hear a question was if it was a novel issue, never ruled upon by the Supreme Court of Texas. I felt that we had two shots at the second avenue which could lead to the granting of the writ and to a hearing. My feeling was that the issue of whether fault in the breakup of the marriage could result in a disproportionate division of the property was an important question for the court. The other question of whether one party's taking care of an adult disabled child could justify a disproportionate division had never been presented to the court. Justice Carver had said in his absurd opinion that Section 3.63 of the Texas Family Code was obviously referring to minor children. The section stated:

> The court shall divide the property of the parties in a manner which is just and right, taking into consideration of each party and any children of the marriage"

I hoped that the court would agree with my position that children, and particularly children who needed special care because of a disability, should be considered by the court. The fact that Mr. Young had done nothing to help Laura or their son for a number of years was a factor in our favor.

I do not think that I have ever been happier about anything in my legal career than reading the letter which informed me that the writ had been granted and that oral argument would be scheduled before the Texas Supreme Court.

I wanted Laura to receive the benefits the trial

46

court had awarded to her and I wanted to maximize her chances with the court. If a writ is granted, the parties are expected to file briefs with the court. If an issue is considered very important by the section of the bar which could encounter the question, an amicus curiae (friend of the court) brief can be filed with the court. I sought out the person I thought could do the best job in Texas of presenting the issues to the Court. She had been my legal writing teacher in law school. She was now working for one of the best family law firms in the state. Reba Graham Rasor agreed to help by writing the amicus brief. The next task was to "shop" the brief for signatures of prominent family law specialists. The annual "Advanced Family Law Course" would prove to be a great place to seek support for our position. The amicus brief ended up being signed by more than fifty family law specialists from all parts of the state.

I was pumped up about having an opportunity to argue before an old acquaintance, Justice Joe Greenhill. The court schedules arguments at eight o'clock in the morning. There may be several cases docketed for that time, so it is necessary to go to Austin the day before the argument in order not to be late for the 8:00 a.m. opening of the session. As the party seeking relief from the court, I was allotted forty-five minutes. I had the right to divide my time however I wanted. The amicus position had no time allotted for a representative to argue their position. I decided to give fifteen minutes to the attorney selected to argue the amicus brief. He was one of the best family lawyers I had ever encountered in my years of practice even up to the present day.

We decided to meet at his hotel room in Austin the evening before the argument to make sure that we were not duplicating our presentations and thus wasting time. I was to be at his hotel room at 8:00 p.m. sharp. I arrived at his hotel and went up to his room. I knocked on the door and waited to be welcomed to work on our presentations. The door opened and it was not the amicus attorney. Instead, it was a gorgeous red-headed young lady, whose blessings were obvious when viewed due to her see through night gown. She smiled and said, "Mr. XXXXX, is not feeling well and he said for me to tell you that he would meet you at the court at 7:30 in the morning." I smiled and replied to her, "Tell Mr. XXXXX that I'm sure that he will be feeling better very soon."

I went back to my hotel and spent several hours going over the briefs and what I planned to say. I made an outline of what I wanted my ailing accomplice to say. I slept very little. The next morning I had a light breakfast and walked across the street to the Supreme Court Building. I arrived about 7:15 and found the courtroom where we would argue. I was about to get an opportunity that many attorneys never get to experience during their entire legal careers. The amicus attorney arrived promptly at 7:30. I inquired about his health and he told me that he had a great night's sleep after taking some medicine. He smiled and said, "Let's kick some butts."

The argument you get to present to the Supreme Court is not an argument in the true sense of the word. The full court would be hearing the arguments. It was not uncommon for the attorney who presented the first argument to be interrupted after the attorney stated his name and whom he represented. You have to try to get back to your presentation as quickly as you can after answering the questions of one or more of the justices to their satisfaction. The session starts with a formal calling of the court to order by the bailiff. "Oyez, Oyez, Oyez, all who have business before this honorable court come forward."

All stand as the Justices enter the chambers and are seated. The bailiff calls the first case for argument and suddenly we are on stage, ready to perform. Chief Justice Greenhill was seated in the center with an equal number of justices on either side of him. I got the shock of my life when Justice Greenhill's first words were, "Mr. Robertson, it is so good to see you again." I had no idea he would remember my invitation to judge the Law School Moot Court finals or remember me. A broad smile spread across the face of the amicus attorney. I responded, "It is an honor to be able to appear before you and this honorable court." What he said next shocked me even more. He asked the opposing attorney to stand. He asked, "Sir, can you tell me why you have utter disregard for the honor and dignity of the Supreme Court of Texas? In all of my years on the court, you are the first attorney who has chosen not to file a brief upon the granting of a writ." Opposing counsel muttered something about how he thought the briefs before the Court of Appeals would be sufficient. It was obvious that it was also his first appearance before the court and he had not made sufficient inquiries as to how things worked.

The Chief Justice has welcomed me and is pissed off at opposing counsel -- how much better can it get? I argued for fifteen minutes with very few interruptions. The amicus attorney followed for fifteen minutes and was great. He answered their questions adroitly. He was followed by the attorney for Mr. Young who was pummeled without mercy for his entire thirty minutes.

My fifteen minute rebuttal followed. Just after I started my argument, Justice Greenhill asked me if I knew why the appellate decision had not mentioned the attorney's fees the trial court had awarded to me. I replied, "Yes, your honor." Here was an opportunity I had dreamed about since Justice Spencer Carver had talked to me after his decision had been issued. Justice Greenhill asked, "Are you going to share what you know with us?" "If you would like, I would be pleased to do so," I answered. He smiled and said," I would like."

"I called Justice Carver and asked why he had not written on the question. He responded that it could be taken care of on remand. I told him I intended to file a writ. He responded, "Just do that, you don't have a snowballs chance in Hell of it being granted."

Justice Pope commented to Justice Greenhill, "Spencer has not learned a thing since law school." The justices laughed and then Justice Greenhill ask me what I thought of a court granting attorney fees when they had not been requested. I responded that I thought it was a really bad idea and a poor precedent for future cases. Justice Greenhill said because it was not a point on appeal, there was nothing the court could do about it.

The argument was over. I thought about something I had done as a kid. I would blow up a balloon as full as I could without it bursting and then turn it loose in my room. It would fly around the room in wild gyrations until all of the air had escaped. It would then lie in a wrinkled mass on the floor, totally spent. I thought that I felt just like that balloon must have felt, if it had the ability to have feelings. My amicus attorney friend and I left the courtroom together. A Southwest flight later, with a few drinks in between, we were back in Dallas. Now we would have to wait on a decision from the court.

Several months later, I received the Texas Supreme Court's decision. The Court of Appeals decision was set aside and the trial court's decision was reinstated. I was elated. My wife and I decided to go to one of our favorite restaurants to celebrate. The restaurant was Ratcliffs, on Cedar Springs in Dallas. We enjoyed dinner, had a fine bottle of wine and followed up with coffee and dessert. After a while, I asked the waiter for the check. He said there is no check. The gentleman in the corner said to tell you congratulations on a great victory for your client and all of the family lawyers who care. I looked over to the corner and saw Ken Fuller. Ken was a true gentleman, a great family lawyer and one of the most caring people whom I have ever met. I waved to him and said thank you. The law had been changed and Laura had received a modicum of the justice she deserved. She paid me five dollars a month for many years after the decision. I figured it cost me about forty thousand dollars to fix what Mr. Young and Justice Carver had caused. Justice Greenhill's words in the opinion he wrote stated, "Being abandoned and not supported for years while she was taking care of their son, daughter and his incontinent mother hardly seem to be nags, bickers or pouts."

Move Over Don Quixote

After Young v. Young, I had the opportunity to work on several more cases which ended up in the Supreme Court of Texas. I had coached sports teams for children since 1961, when I started coaching in the Park Cities YMCA program for the elementary schools. I was coaching the Armstrong Elementary School fifth grade boys' basketball team. The father of one of the players was an attorney. He had been seriously injured in an accident. The truck driver who caused the wreck had violated a traffic signal and run over my player's father. The father was in a body cast for a number of months. He had multiple fractures and was unable to work or do anything of much use around the house.

Months after the accident, he settled his case for the policy limits of the defendant's insurance policy. When he told his wife of the settlement, she asked what she received in the settlement. He explained that under Texas law, the wife had no right to sue for damages when someone negligently injures her husband. His wife was very upset. He called and asked me to talk to her and calm her down about her lack of a remedy for what she perceived to be unfair treatment under the law. The law in Texas had always allowed the husband to sue for loss of consortium of his wife due to the negligent actions of a third party. Consortium is defined as wifely services, including housekeeping and sexual services. There was no comparable right on the part of the wife to sue for loss of consortium of her husband. The husband wanted me to explain the law and how she had no rights under law. I agreed to talk to her. Prior to our conference, I reviewed the law, including the

Texas Equal Rights Amendment for women which had been passed in 1967. I figured that the common law right on the part of the husband to sue for loss of consortium plus the Equal Rights Amendment created the wife's right to sue for loss of consortium of the husband. My conclusion was not what the husband wanted to hear.

My partner, Ron Wilkinson, filed suit on behalf of the wife. The wife was not interested in a big recovery. As a matter of principle, she wanted to establish her right to sue for loss of consortium. The wife's case was dismissed when a motion for summary judgment was granted against her by a judge best known for his collection of Snoopy dolls. He was the same judge who had presided over the "Court of Inquiry" which I will describe later. The Dallas Court of Appeals set aside the summary judgment and the defendant appealed. The wife had offered to settle for a nominal sum as long as the settlement recognized her rights. Had the defendant settled, there would never been a written decision which could be considered as legal precedent. The law professor who was associated to work on the case made it clear that the defendant would not settle, even for a nickel. The Supreme Court granted the writ filed by the insurance company, but ruled in favor of our client. As a result of the decision, every workman's compensation case and every personal injury case involving injuries to the husband filed after the Supreme Court's decision, has included a count for loss of consortium. The wife felt vindicated, but I am not sure how her husband felt about the resolution of the matter. It was the second victory for women's rights the firm had before the Texas Supreme Court, but not the last.

Common Law Marriage

Texas had always recognized common law marriage. When the Family Code became effective on January 1, 1970, the term "common law marriage" was eliminated and the term "informal marriage" came into existence. It was one of the many terms which were changed by the drafters of the Family Code. I have never decided whether there was any reason for the changing of the terms other than just being different from the other states.

In order to prove the existence of an "informal marriage," you had to show that three elements had been met. First, you had to show that the parties had cohabited. Second, you had to show that the parties had held themselves out to be husband and wife to others. Third, you had to show that the parties had agreed to be married. The problem with defending allegations of the existence of a common law marriage was that the third element, agreement to be married, could be inferred from a combination of the first two, cohabitation and holding out as husband and wife.

My prospective client had been referred to me, not by my client, but by my client's former spouse. I was always flattered when the referrals came from former opponents. He explained that he had been sued for divorce by his former live-in girlfriend. They had broken up over three years before she sued him for divorce. They had never been engaged nor had they ever gone through the process of getting a marriage license or having a wedding ceremony. At the time of their break-up, he was unemployed and "didn't have enough money to pay attention."

After the split, he had become involved in an oil and gas exploration venture as a salesman of partnership interests in the project. He had received a "carried interest" in the project in exchange for his sales efforts. The project was very successful as were a number of other ventures in which he owned a carried interest. He had gone from the outhouse to the penthouse in just three years. He surmised that his former girlfriend had heard about his success and wanted a piece of the action.

I informed him about the existence of informal marriage in Texas and quizzed him at length about the factors which could be relevant in determining whether or not he was married. He admitted that they had traveled together under his name and had taken advantage of some fares by buying tickets as husband and wife. Hotel reservations had been made as Mr. and Mrs. as had car rentals and restaurant reservations. There was no doubt that they had cohabited for several years.

The reported facts were not looking good if one's goal was to defend your client against the allegation of informal marriage. I took a break to try to think about looking at the situation from a different perspective. I remembered how I had been able to help the little lady who had been the cook at the white house. She had prevailed because there had been an impediment to the other possible widow's legal marriage. You cannot get legally married if you are already married to someone else.

I went back into my office and asked, "Did you ever live with another woman before you lived with the one who has sued you for divorce?" He replied, "Sure, I lived with another girl for several years." I pressed him, "did you travel with her, make reservations and buy tickets with her as your wife?" When he replied that they had done all of the same things and even had credit cards and a checking account together, I saw a huge light at the end of the tunnel. "Was your break-up friendly?"

He explained that they were still friends and had dinner together from time to time. "Have you ever considered that you might be married to her, instead of the girl who has sued you for divorce?" "How would that make a difference?" he asked. I told him that if he was married to the first live-in girlfriend, he couldn't be legally married to the girl who had sued him for divorce. He smiled broadly. He said that he needed to call the first lady and have a serious talk with her. I excused myself as he was dialing her number.

After a quite a few minutes, he came out of my office looking for me. We went back into my office and he said, "You are going to need to file a divorce action for me." "I talked to the first lady and we agreed that we are married."

A divorce petition was filed on his behalf with the first live-in lady as the respondent. She had her attorney file an answer, admitting the existence of the marriage. I filed an answer in the first case, setting up the existence of the marriage as a defense against the first filed suit, which was dismissed. The decree of divorce was agreed to by the parties and the divorce was granted after the sixty day waiting period. The property division was not contested.

I understood that the now ex-wife had selected a metallic gold color for her new Jaguar Vanden Plas. My client sent me a picture of the brass plaque he had attached to the front door of his house on Beverly Drive.

It read:
"THIS IS THE HOME OF A SINGLE MAN, WHO INTENDS TO STAY THAT WAY."

The Tire Was a Pirelli

The video tape was over and my case was finished. All you could see in the last frame of the video tape was Pirelli. It was displayed in bold letters on a tire mounted on one of Enzo Ferrari's magnificent red beasts. How the tire came to capture the last scene of the video is one of my favorite stories.

The case started out on a great note. My distraught potential client had brought a recent financial statement and several tax returns. She was sobbing softly while trying to tell me about her long-term marriage coming apart at the seams. Her husband was a self-made man who had risen to the top of his industry with hard work and an alert mind. The couple had gone from having very little to having an overabundance of everything. Divorce lawyers love cases which do not have contested issues regarding children but do have a great deal of property to divide. She thought about when they had started to grow apart and blamed it on everything but herself. It is very common to externalize problems to help from facing the reality that both parties are almost always contributors to the death of a marriage. Few--if any--divorces are the fault of just one of the parties.

My preference in cases which principally involve property issues is to file suit, but not have the spouse served by a sheriff, constable or private process server. I learned long ago that a frontal attack on someone who had built a thriving business was a sure-fire way to get lumps on your head. Starting a case in a confrontational way is almost never in your client's best interests.

Dealing with hard-headed, strong-willed people is an art. You can almost always accomplish more by asking questions rather than making statements.

The financial statement and tax returns told me that the case would present the interesting challenge of how to make a fair division of the property in the most tax-effective way. We had a stroke of good luck when the husband hired an attorney who was very capable, honest and willing to be creative in how we dealt with the assets and liabilities. The parties' accountant agreed to work with us to craft a property division which met the needs of the parties. Most of the time the wife wants security and liquidity to be at the top of her wish list. The husband often wants control of the business or assets which he has managed and is willing to take more risks if he has a chance of greater rewards.

Everything was going swimmingly until my client was served with notice to have her deposition taken by opposing counsel A deposition is a proceeding where one attorney asks questions of the other party who is under oath to tell the truth. Depositions can be videotaped if requested by the attorney asking the questions. I wondered why my client was being deposed and why the deposition was being videotaped. When asked, the opposing attorney responded that there were just a few things he needed to clear up. My client professed total ignorance of why her husband might want to have her deposed. I had an unpleasant feeling that my client was not leveling with me.

The deposition was scheduled to be taken in my conference room several weeks later. I prepared my client for deposition by reviewing the rules for asking and answering question. Many clients think they have to present their position at the deposition. That is just not true. The purpose for taking a deposition is threefold. The first purpose is to find facts from the person being deposed. The second purpose is for the attorney taking the deposition to assess what kind of witness the person will be if the case goes to trial. The third purpose is to limit testimony if the case goes to trial. An example would be to ask, "Tell me all of the reasons you believe you should receive more than fifty percent of the property." At trial, the witness could be limited to those reasons during testimony. It is important to add to any question which may be intended to limit testimony, "that is all I can think of at this time." I thought the review had gone well.

The reporter who would be taking the testimony and the videographer arrived about thirty minutes early to set up their equipment in the conference room. About fifteen minutes later the husband and his attorney arrived. I knew the attorney and had seen the picture of the husband on television and in the newspaper, but I did not realize he was such a large man. He was at least six-foot four inches tall and weighed 250 or more. He was ruggedly handsome. My client was an attractive, tall blonde woman who was obviously in great physical condition. I thought that the two made a handsome couple.

My client was sworn in by the reporter and the attorney started asking questions. Basic background questions were asked with no surprises until the husband's attorney asked me if he could use my screen which could be lowered out of the ceiling. I had no idea about what was going to happen, but agreed for him to use the screen. Now is the time for me to share what I found out after the fact so that you will understand the impact, no pun intended, of the video. It seems as though my client, after having become disenchanted with her husband over a period of years, had found a new romantic interest in her life. The fact that she had not shared that information with me did not make me a "happy camper." A good attorney can deal with anything he knows about, but he is hard put to handle negative surprises. I discovered that my client had been meeting her new romantic interest in the parking lot of Preston Center East. For those of you who do not know North Dallas, that section of the Preston Center shopping center really lost tenants when Neiman-Marcus closed their store. There were isolated parts of Preston Center East where no shops were open. The sidewalks and parking areas had many large live oak trees which had grown quite dense due to a lack of needed thinning of the interior branches. The husband's attorney had hired a private detective to follow my client. The husband's suspicions had been verified by the private detective.

Several times per week my client would drive her big Cadillac to the most remote part of the parking area and stop right in front of a huge live oak tree. Several minutes later she would be joined by a handsome man driving a bright red Ferrari. He would get out of his car and join my client in her car. After a period of hot kissing and groping, their visit would be concluded by my client giving her friend oral sex in the front seat of the Cadillac. The husband only cared about his wife's conduct because it could greatly affect the judge's property division. Our judge thought of herself as the "Avenging Angel." Inappropriate sexual conduct could cost you big bucks in her court. There exists a myth in Texas that property is automatically divided fifty-fifty in divorce cases. That has never been the law in Texas. The standard is that property will be divided in a manner that is just and right, taking into consideration the rights of both parties. A laundry list of factors is considered by the judge in making a division. The judge has great discretion and is seldom, if ever, reversed by the higher court if the matter is appealed. The list of factors would have heavily favored my client, but for the "fellatio in the front seat."

The husband wanted better proof of what was going on with the well-tanned driver of the Ferrari. The attorney talked the private detective into climbing up into the dense branches of the live oak tree to film the now expected repeat performance. On the first trip up into the tree nothing happened. Undaunted, the next day the investigator dutifully climbed up into the dense branches and waited for the anticipated encounter. Voila! Here came the Cadillac, followed a few minutes later by the monster red Ferrari. What followed could have been scripted by the writer for an XXXX-rated movie. After a brief interlude of kissing and more groping, her blouse and bra came off. A short time later she began her usual method of pleasing her lover. The private detective had a great view of the proceedings which were all being filmed with his video camera. What happened next could have been caused by several different factors. He could have just lost his balance; maybe a squirrel startled him. In any event, he came crashing down out of the tree on to the hood of the Cadillac. The camera never stopped filming. It bounced off of the hood onto the ground and came to rest aimed at the name Pirelli on the tire of the Ferrari. There was a considerable amount of scrambling after the thud on the hood. The private detective was lying on the sidewalk clutching his camera, the Cadillac screeched off and the loud roar of the Ferrari left in the opposite direction.

The deposition was recessed and I visited with opposing counsel in the small conference room. The case settled about twenty minutes after the deposition had recessed. We had lost all hope for a disproportionate division. The lover has appeared in several other cases I know about. I think of him and my client every time I hear the very identifiable roar of a Ferrari.

LAW SCHOOL

My First Year

It was in late August, 1966 and I was having a difficult time getting back into studying after my mind had vegetated for two years in the Air Force. Contracts, Torts, Property, Criminal Law, Legal Writing and Legal History comprised the menu for the first semester. Our class had one hundred and twenty men and only six women.

The Colonel

My first experience with professors in law school was an eye opener. The first week of class I was introduced to the "Socratic Method." The teacher would call on a student who would stand and be asked questions for an indeterminate period of time. Some of the professors seemed to be invested in humiliating the students more than encouraging learning. Professor Arthur Harding, who was called "Colonel Harding," taught Contracts. He had gone to Harvard Law School and had taken Contracts from Professor Williston. If any of you saw the movie, "The Paper Chase," the law professor in the movie was modeled after Professor Williston. Colonel Harding thought he was Williston. If he gave a damn about any of the students, I never saw an indication of it in the two semesters I was in his class. However, he did provide two of the most vivid memories of my time in law school.

It was the first day of class. The classroom had been renovated and was a new a theater style lecture hall. The rows of tables where the students sat sloped steeply from the stage-like platform where the professor lectured. The arrangement was new to the students and the professors. Everyone was scared to death that he would be the Colonel's first victim. When the first student's name was called out, he stood on shaky legs looking down at his notes. As the Colonel began his famous slicing and dicing questions, he was pacing back and forth across the new platform. He was talking and not watching where he was on the platform when he stepped off of the platform into a metal trash can. Rather than step down into the can and possibly fall, he kicked the metal can toward the wall which was about ten feet away. The student who was responding to his questions was looking down at his notes and did not see what was happening on the stage. When the metal can hit the wall of the classroom, it sounded like a cannon shot. The student, who was reciting, fainted. That is how my law school career started.

We learned quickly that the Colonel couldn't see far past his nose. He had a seating chart which he used with the names of the students in large print. It became a regular practice for members of the class to sit in seats other than the ones assigned to them. It was either the second or third week when the Colonel called on the person who sat next to me. We were seated alphabetically in rows. Many of the people in my row had names starting with R or S. In a loud voice, the Colonel called out, "Mr. R." There was no answer from my classmate seated next to me who was not Mr. R. In an even louder voice, Colonel Harding boomed out, "Mr. R." Once again, the fellow seated next to me did not respond. The Colonel was getting noticeably irritated, and in an even louder voice asked, "If you are not Mr. R, then who the hell are you?" My classmate rose from his chair, gathered his books and responded to the Colonel, "Fat Chance." He then walked up the stairs out of the lecture hall and immediately became a class hero. The Colonel never discovered the identity of "Fat Chance."

Professor Harding was very intelligent. His ego was the size of Mt. Everest. I decided that God must have put him on earth to teach us how not to treat our fellow man. That is about all I learned from his class in Contracts.

Clyde Emery

Our Property professor in my first year was Clyde Emery. He cared about us and wanted to help us be good lawyers. He was somewhat of a physical fitness nut. He rode his bicycle to school for years from six miles away. He wore a shirt and tie, topped by a sweater, topped by a sport coat or suit coat. He was seventy years old during my first year in law school. On his seventieth birthday, our class got him a cake with seventy candles which you could not blow out. I was afraid that we might kill him, as he would not accept that he could not blow out the candles.

He almost always wore a hat when not indoors. He believed that heat and energy flowed from one's head unless it was covered by a hat. He had a rowing machine in his office along with a curious device he had built which had a heater and a fan. He had several hats which he would alternate between the top of the heater/fan and his head.

Professor Emery was a brilliant attorney who invented the "Key Number System" which made legal research much easier and more precise. He told us to call him any time we had a property law question with which he could help us. I took him up on his offer several times both before and after graduation.

Joseph Webb McKnight

Professor McKnight was my favorite teacher. He had more degrees than any other professor. He taught first year students "Legal History." Most of us called it Legal Mystery. Professor McKnight used a textbook titled "History and Origins of the Common Law" by H.M.S. Fifoot, a portion of which was written in Latin. The first day of class, Professor McKnight called on me. I confessed that I was having a bit of trouble deciphering the portion of the text that was in Latin. He asked the class, "How many other unfortunates are there in this class who never took Latin?" I tried not to take the remark personally. I really liked Joe McKnight and took every course he taught, including family law, marital property and a seminar in legal ethics. He proved to be a valuable resource throughout my career and was always willing to help me with interesting and unusual problems. The four courses I took from Joe McKnight were the most enjoyable ones in my three years of school.

While I was in law school, Professor McKnight was working on the "Family Code Project" along with attorney Louise Raggio and Eugene Smith, another professor. Their work changed family law in Texas and put all family code into one volume which made it much easier to locate and understand. Texas divorce law changed from requiring an allegation of adultery or physical cruelty to having seven grounds for divorce, three of which were "No Fault" grounds.

Joe viewed things from an unusual perspective.

Sometimes he didn't consider the practical implications of his words or actions. For example, Professor McKnight wrote a good deal of Title One of the Texas Family Code, which was titled "Husband and Wife." Chapter One, Section 1.01 was titled 'Marriage License," and originally read:

Persons desiring to enter into a ceremonial marriage shall obtain a marriage license from the county clerk of any county of this state.

Title One became effective on January 1, 1970. The new code provision had deleted the words "A man and a woman" and replaced them with "Persons." On the first day the county clerk's office was open after January 1, 1970, a significant number of same-sex couples were lined up to get marriage licenses. I am positive that Professor McKnight never anticipated the consequences of the change in wording of the statute. Unintentionally, Texas was the first state in the nation which did not have a prohibition against same-sex marriage. The county clerk refused to issue marriage licenses to same-sex couples and the Texas Attorney General wrote an opinion which stated that the statute meant "a man and a woman." The next legislative session, in 1971, the language was restored to "a man and a woman" and a sentence was added which stated, "A license may not be issued for the marriage of persons of the same sex."

Joe drove an early 1950's era maroon Mercury the entire time I was in law school and for years thereafter. He was of average height and had an un-athletic build. There was an air of dignity about him despite his sometimes rumpled suit and his ever present handkerchief. He had gone to Oxford to acquire one of his many degrees. He was never in doubt about his keen intellect. One might interpret his actions to be somewhat pompous, but Joe had a heart of gold.

I was fortunate to be selected as a member of the Family Law Council several years after my graduation from law school. The Council met several times per year at various locations around the state. One of the most memorable meetings occurred in El Paso. Although our hotel was in El Paso, we spent a good amount of time in Juarez, just across the border in Mexico. One night we decided to have dinner at the "Dog Track" in Juarez. You could have a tasty dinner and watch and bet on greyhound races. Our very attractive waitresses not only served us our dinner and drinks, but also took our bets and returned our winnings, if any. I had consumed at least four margaritas when Eugene Smith noticed that Joe McKnight was sitting at a table by himself in the corner of the section where we were all seated. Gene bellowed out, "Joe, aren't you having a good time?" Joe responded as only he could, "I cannot believe that all of you derive pleasure from betting on dumb animals."

That should give you a glimpse into the thinking of Joe McKnight. Later he called me to say that he was going to Spain to work on a book on the influence of Spanish law on Texas law. He asked if I would be interested in teaching his class in the Masters of Liberal Arts program at Southern Methodist University while he was gone. The course was called "The Family and the Law." It was a survey course about family law which was taught to candidates seeking a master's degree. I was excited about the possibility of teaching on a graduate school level.

I taught the course for several years and really enjoyed teaching and interacting with the students. It was a pleasure to work with teachers who were interested in family law because of the number of the children in their classes whose parents were either divorced or divorcing. They wanted to understand the law so that they could do a better job of helping their students who were facing the realities of their parents changing marital status. I also had graduate students in psychology, sociology and theology who wanted to broaden their understanding of the dynamics of the divorce process. There would always be several students who were contemplating the possibility of divorce in the future. They would be there to learn how property might be divided in their own divorce, or how much child support might be ordered. The other students, who signed up for the course, were assistant coaches in the athletic programs at SMU. Many of my students were motivated to get their master's degree in order to get a raise in pay.

When Professor McKnight returned from his sabbatical in Spain, we had lunch at Kuby's, one of our favorite places near the law school. During our discussion, I told him that my wife and I would be going to England the next summer for a vacation and a visit with her English relatives. Joe suggested that I meet his Oxford University roommate, Sir Anthony Walton, who was a member of the House of Lords. I was excited about the prospects of meeting a member of the House of Lords and possibly getting a tour of the law courts and the upper house of parliament. The arrangements were made and came to fruition the next summer. Sir Anthony was gracious and impressive. He gave me a tour which I will never forget. At the conclusion of the day's activities, when I was thanking Sir Anthony for his kindness in giving me the opportunity to experience that which was not available to tourists, he made a most confusing request. He asked me to ask Joe, "How are you and GA getting on?" I confessed that I did not understand the question. He explained in the first week that he and Joe were classmates at Oxford; the students were divided into study groups of six members. Joe had refused to participate in a study group, exclaiming, "I have everything to offer and nothing to gain." Sir Anthony explained that the joke among their classmates was that, Joe and God Almighty, GA, had their own study group. Upon our return to Dallas, I scheduled another lunch with Joe at Kuby's. After we had finished lunch and I had thanked Joe for the introduction, I said, "Sir Anthony asked how you and GA were getting on;" The look on Joe's face was priceless. He said, "You must never tell a living soul that story." That I have not honored Professor Joe McKnight's request is obvious. He helped me throughout my legal career.

Moot Court

When I started law school, first year students were required to participate in Moot Court. The class was divided into groups of eight students who worked with an upperclassman. Each person had a partner who helped make up four, two man teams. Every year a problem would be presented to the participants which involved a currently disputed legal question. You and your partner had to prepare to argue either side of the question. At the end of the semester, a competition was held among all of the participants to determine which team had done the best job of arguing the issue. In the competition, you might have to argue one position in the first round, only to have to argue the opposite side in the next round. I really enjoyed Moot Court because it gave us our first chance to prepare and argue a case against other teams of our classmates. My partner was totally disinterested in the program and announced to me that we should try and lose in the first round and be rid of the time-consuming activity. He got his wish as we lost in the first round of the competition. I was recruited to fill in for another team when one of the members had to leave town to be with a sick parent. I think that I was the only person to be on two losing teams during the same year.

The Dean announced that Moot Court would not be continued as a law school sponsored course the next year. Seven of us got together and created what we called the Moot Court Board. We asked the Dean if the program could be continued as a student taught course. I will never forget his words: He said, "Every tub must sit on its own bottom," whatever the hell that meant. I asked him if we could continue the program provided at least 25% of the incoming class signed up to participate. He responded that we couldn't get 20% to sign up. I said I have a twenty dollar bill that says we will get more than your 20%. He agreed to the bet. The next fall we got almost 80% of the incoming first year students to sign up. The Dean welched on his bet for two years. When I was a second semester third year student I had to take Secured Transactions, which was taught by the Dean. After the last lecture and before the class was dismissed, he asked if anyone had any questions. I raised my hand and asked him if he was ever going to pay me the money he had lost in our bet. He angrily got out his check book and wrote me a check for $20.00. I endorsed it to the Law School Fund and handed it back to him. He was really pissed. He gave me my lowest grade in law school, but passed me. That

$20.00 was my last gift to the law school until he retired.

A Bushel of Peaches

When it came time to look for a summer clerkship or law related job, I decided to try to work for a public law agency one year, a larger law firm the next year and a small law firm the summer I was to take the bar exam. The first summer, I was an intern at the Dallas Legal Services Project, a program sponsored by the Office of Economic Opportunity War on Poverty. There were four law students from SMU working there that summer. Beverly Neblett, David Snodgrass, Stan Huller and I worked on different projects for staff attorneys. The project director was an attorney who had never practiced law. The staff attorneys were exceptional. Maxine McConnell and Walter Steele became faculty members at SMU School of Law.

The Project was opening a much needed community office on Metropolitan Street in South Dallas, which was a minority area inhabited principally by blacks. I was told that I would supervise a crew of young men who had been hired to hand out circulars in the surrounding neighborhoods, announcing the opening of the new office. I had grown up in a Federal housing project in West Oak Cliff and had some knowledge about where one could go safely in other parts of town. Kids from West Dallas were not welcome in South Dallas for example. The crew that was hired to deliver circulars in South Dallas consisted totally of boys from West Dallas. We went to South Dallas in a good-sized van. Shortly after we arrived at the new neighborhood office on Metropolitan Street, a group of local boys started to gather around us. I got the crew back in the van and drove to the farmer's market, which was on the north edge of South Dallas. I bought a bushel of peaches, put them in the van and headed back to the South Dallas office with my crew. I told them to stay in the van and I approached the local kids. I explained why we were there and what we wanted to do to help their neighborhood with the legal services office. I told them that even though I asked for guys from their neighborhood, I had been given six boys from West Dallas. I told them to pick six guys who wanted to help us deliver the circulars and I would pay them half of the money I had been given. But first I had a bushel of peaches for us all to eat and get to know each other. It worked, the circulars were delivered and the new legal services office helped the neighborhood.

Undercover Assignment

If you think that was a tense situation, you ain't heard nothing yet. My next assignment took almost all summer. I worked under cover. One of the lead attorneys, Walter Steele, had reason to believe that a scam was being run on poor people, resulting in their having fraudulent liens filed on their homes. Advertisements in the local papers under the names "Mister Cash" or "Mister Green" offered to loan money to persons in need. When people called to inquire about borrowing money, they would be asked if they had made any repairs to their houses, such as a new roof, fence or interior improvements. If they responded that they had, they would be told that for their loan to be approved, they would have to come to an office to get the money. When they arrived at the office, they would be presented with papers to sign.

After they left, the papers they had signed were taken into another room with a shadow box. This is a device that has window-pane-like glass with a strong light under the glass. Signatures on the loan documents would be traced on to papers stating the money was loaned to pay for the repairs or improvements, which allowed liens to be filed. If the borrowers did not pay according to the loan documents, foreclosure procedures would be filed to take away the borrowers' homes.

My cover was that I was doing a survey for the Better Business Bureau. My job was to interview the borrowers we had identified who had liens filed on their property. Everything was going well until the lenders, whose money was coming from Las Vegas and New Jersey, caught wind of the survey. We suspected that the bad guys were on to us so I had been given a body guard. His name was Willie. He was a very large black man who had played some professional football before he tore up a knee. I became very fond of Willie, although he ate like a horse. I was given money to cover some expenses, but it was never enough to cover the costs of Willie's lunches. His lunch would be two double meat cheeseburgers, two orders of fries and a six-pack of cokes.

Willie always waited in the car while I talked to people being "surveyed." I had a briefcase which contained a reel-to-reel recorder. The recorder turned on when I moved the briefcase handle. I was interviewing a couple and recording the conversation when the tape slipped off of the reel and started going ka-thump, ka-thump, ka-thump. Two guys came quickly out of the back room and I took off like a shot with them on my tail. I ran and jumped through the open left front window of my 1964 Chevrolet. The noise woke up Willie, who was sleeping in the back seat. He got out of the car, just as the two fellows chasing me got there. Wonderful Willie asked them, "Is there something I can do for you guys?" Willie was about 6'4" and probably weighed close to 300 pounds. The two thugs beat a hasty retreat. Willie got back in the car I took off like I was at the Yellow Belly Drag Strip in Grand Prairie, where we raced our cars on the weekends.

The investigation had produced hard evidence that a fraudulent scheme was causing poor people across Dallas to lose their homes. One method of exposing the wrong was to convene a "Court of Inquiry." Courts of Inquiry are unique to Texas. No other state has such a procedure. The presiding administrative judge in a judicial district has the power to appoint one of the district judges to convene the inquiry and appoint an attorney to be the court's representative. The attorney who was appointed was short and fat with black curly hair and an ever present bow tie around his neck. He was smart and clever and was never taken lightly by his adversaries. He and the judge appointed to conduct the inquiry were old buddies.

Things were going badly for the finance company which fronted the money to be loaned to the poor folks. After several days of testimony and evidence, I was sure that indictments would follow. The Court of Inquiry has no power to bring criminal indictments or to try those believed to be violating the law. If irregularities are found, the matter is referred to the Grand Jury or to another court. The next morning a new attorney showed up representing the finance company. He was one of the most powerful lawyers in the state, having political influence from Austin to Washington, D.C. and back. He had been a classmate of one of the top officials in state government while in law school. He also represented one of the largest religious denominations in the state. Shortly after he appeared, the judge announced that there would be a conference in his chambers of all of the lawyers involved in the case. I wondered what was going on and waited in the courtroom.

More than an hour later, the judge in charge and the attorneys came back. The judge announced that the Court of Inquiry was being shut down. Most of the illegally filed liens were removed from the records and. many poor folks who had borrowed money did not lose their homes. I never learned what really happened in the judge's office. I did learn that it is not *what* you know; it is *who* you know that often determines the outcome of litigation.

My Second Year

Jan P Charmatz

My second year of law school was more enjoyable than my first. I had gotten back into the swing of studying a bit and understood more about how to do well in school. It was in my second year that I encountered another favorite professor, Jan P. Charmatz. He had been a law professor at the University of Prague, in Czechoslovakia, before World War II. I was told that in exchange for serving as a prosecutor at the Nuremberg war crime trials he was given American citizenship and the rank of major in the United States Army. He assisted in the prosecution of Albert Speer, the architect who helped provide armaments for the German army. Speer received a twenty-year prison sentence. He corresponded with Professor Charmatz while he was in prison and while I was in school.

My professor was probably the favorite of most of the law students. He was the only one who would drink with us and always provided a good time when he socialized with his students. On one occasion he was accused of using offensive language around female class members. He proclaimed that at his age, all he could ever be charged with would be "assault with a dead weapon." During the summers he would help write constitutions for emerging nations. He was one of the few professors who really cared for the students, whether or not you were in his class. During my third year he participated in an event which will live in my memory forever. But I am getting ahead of myself, so I will return to 1967-68.

I was elected to be a member of the Student Bar Association. I enjoyed Moot Court, activities with the Student Bar and most of my courses. My wife was doing well in her job. I took her to work in the morning and picked her up in the afternoon so I had use of our only car during the day. I did not study much during my second year. I was in the top half of my class, but not doing as well as I should have been if I had worked a little harder.

Tobolosky, Schlinger and Blaylock

Toward the middle of the spring semester I started worrying about a summer clerkship. I applied for a position with a downtown Dallas law firm. There were three partners who were all well respected in the Dallas legal community. On the day of the interviews I looked at the other candidates for the clerkship. They all ranked higher in my class than I did. My chances didn't look good. After the interviews we were told that we would be notified by the end of the week. To my great surprise, I was offered the job. I quickly accepted and was scheduled to work a few hours each week until the summer break. On one of my first days at work I asked the senior partner why I had been selected over the other candidates. He explained that I had been selected because he thought I was the strongest candidate. I did not realize that he meant physically strongest! He had a withered arm. He explained that a client of the firm was buying about twenty-five movie theaters. The contracts for the closing were expected to weigh close to one hundred pounds and would be in two large cases. He could not carry the cases due to his arm. I was expected to go with him to Beaumont to the closing of the transaction. I was 6'2" and weighed about 185 at that time.

Regardless of the reason I was hired, it was a wonderful place to work. I learned a great deal about business law and even more about how to practice law. They offered me a job when I graduated. Two of the senior partners were Jewish. Most of their principal clients were also Jewish. One of the partners had suffered a serious heart attack during my third year. The other partner was also having health problems. I was afraid that their Jewish clients would change firms if the two partners were not there. I accepted another job offer.

Fortunately, both of the fine gentlemen lived many years and one, Henry Schlinger, later became the president of the

Dallas Bar Association. Two things happened while I was working there that taught me lessons which have served me well over the years of my practice.

Edwin Tobolosky, the partner who interviewed me and hired me to be his "mule" had two things he expected me to do every week. The first was to keep the refrigerator stocked with soft drinks, which was fine with me. The second was to work every Saturday answering the phone, a job I complained about on a fairly regular basis. I could study or work on firm business as long as I was there to answer the phone. There were some Saturdays when the phone might ring twice during the whole day.

The enjoyable part of working on Saturdays was having breakfast with one of the legendary lawyers in the Dallas Bar Association. Morris Jaffe. He was a partner in the highly respected firm Wynne, Jaffe and Tinsley and he, too, worked on Saturday mornings. Talking to him at breakfast was an educational treat. After breakfast, I took the elevator in the Southland Center up to the office for my 8 to 5 Saturday shift answering the phone. I started each Saturday by filling the refrigerator with soft drinks. The one Saturday which still remains vivid in my mind, a client and the firm were helped beyond my wildest imagination.

About thirty minutes before I could go home the phone rang. I answered, "Attorney's office; how may I help you?" There was a hysterical woman on the phone. She was crying and sobbing as she told me her husband had been killed in a plane crash. I called Mr. Tobolosky on another line while keeping lady's line open. Mr. T answered the phone. I conferenced the two calls and he took over. I later learned that her husband was a surgeon. The doctor was on flight from Houston to Dallas and it had crashed in a thunderstorm. An attorney in the firm was sent to her house to help her. She hired the firm to represent her negligence suit which would be huge. Mr. Tobolosky brought in an expert airline crash attorney, who would later serve on the Texas Supreme Court.

The Monday after the case had been signed up on the

previous Saturday, I received word Mr. Tobolosky wanted see me. I had no idea what he wanted. I sat down in the client chair across the desk from his big leather chair. He smiled broadly and said, "Now do you understand why you answer the phone on Saturday?" He reminded me of a poem by John Milton, which I've never forgotten. He said, "They also serve who only stand and wait."

The summer of 1968 at Tobolosky, Schlinger and Blaylock was a great experience. An event which would match the airplane crash case occurred during mid-summer. I was walking down the hall when I heard crying from one of the offices. The door was not completely closed and I peered inside. One of the associates had his head down on his desk sobbing. I stuck my head in the door and asked, "Is there anything I can do to help?" His response was, "I'm going to be fired." "Why?" I asked. He continued sobbing and told me that the statute of limitations had run while the file was sitting on his desk. In Texas, you have the right to sue the other party for four years from the date of the contract. Failure to file suit within the four-year period causes the plaintiff to lose the right to sue based upon the contract.

The associate was supposed to have filed the lawsuit for breach of contract and had failed to do so. The amount of money involved in the dispute was substantial. The possibility of the firm being sued by the client was great.

We represented a Hong Kong clothing manufacturer who purchased hundreds of bales of cotton from a Texas company. The cotton had been sold as "good" quality. The grades of cotton, from worst to best are poor, fair, middling, good and excellent. When our client got ready to weave the cotton into cloth, all the bales were tested. Only a few were "good"; most of them were "fair." I had heard the expression "fair to middling," but never really understood the meaning until I worked on this case. I asked the associate if I could read the contract. He said, "Sure but it's too late to do anything." I did not have a specific assignment that day, so I found a quiet place and started reading. I had read about two-thirds of the contract when I found an interesting statement I did not understand.

"If there's a dispute as to the quality of the cotton, it will be determined under the Liverpool Rules of Arbitration."

I had no idea what the Liverpool Rules of Arbitration were, but I knew who would know. I told the associate to cover for me and left for the SMU Law School. I arrived at the Law School and went directly to the faculty offices. Joe McKnight was in his office and invited me to enter. I asked, "Do you know anything about the Liverpool Rules of Arbitration?" "Of course, I have a copy of them in the library basement" he responded. I did not know the library had a basement, let alone two floors of basement filled with books and other legal documents. On the way to the innards of the library, Joe asked, "Why do you want to know about the Liverpool Rules?" I explained the problem of limitations and the statement about quality being determined under the Liverpool Rules. "You're going to be very pleased" he responded. After Joe located the rules we sat down at a table to look at the contract and the rules.

A contract is considered "sealed" when it contains a seal set in wax. The Liverpool rules stated the statute of limitations on quality disputes is six years on an unsealed contract and twelve years if the contract is sealed. Our contract was not sealed, so we had six years not four to file the action. I got a copy of the rules and headed back downtown. I rushed the associate's office and proclaimed, "You are saved, under the Liverpool rules the statute of limitations is six years, not four." I feared for a moment that I might be kissed by the 6'5" two hundred and fifty pound associate. "Joe McKnight had a copy of the rules and helped me analyze contract." "What do we owe him?" the associate asked. I told him a half-gallon of Chevis Regal. "Cheap at twice the price" he responded and announced, "I have a pleading I have to draft right now."

The lawsuit was filed a later that week. A prominent firm answered the suit with the request the suit be dismissed because the four year statute of limitations had run. It was obvious that the Defendant's attorney did not know about the Liverpool Rules of Arbitration either. At the hearing on the motion to dismiss the associate introduced a copy of the Liverpool Rules into evidence. The judge denied the motion to dismiss and instructed the attorneys to follow the procedures of the Liverpool Rules to determine the dispute. The cotton was not of the quality represented at the time of sale. Our client prevailed. The associate left the firm several years later and started his own firm which was highly successful. He thanked me many times during our legal careers for helping in his time of need.

MORE CASES

Airline Adventures

The Bumpy Flight

I have represented a number of airline pilots and flight attendants over the years. I have represented an equal number of spouses of airline pilots and flight attendants. Divorce seems to be indigenous to the people in the airline industry. I always ask each pilot and flight attendant to share their most interesting stories with me before their cases are concluded. I will share some with you starting with the "Bumpy Flight."

One of my pilot clients told me of an occurrence on a flight from Dallas to Washington D. C. The story was gleaned from information from flight attendants, passengers and the personal observations of the pilot.

A red-headed, freckled-faced, ten-year-old boy boarded the flight in Dallas. He was on the way to spend part of the summer with his father who lived outside of Washington D.C. in northern Virginia. Airlines do a great job taking care of children who fly unaccompanied by an adult. A flight attendant is usually assigned to keep an eye on each child and take care of any special needs they might have. The flight attendant assigned to the boy, whom I will call Huck, showed him to his seat and helped him get his carry-on bag under his seat. It was a bag like a guy would use to carry gym shoes and work-out gear.

Every few minutes, Huck would take the bag from under the seat, unzip the top just a little way and peer into the bag. After the flight attendant had witnessed him doing this a number of times, she asked him if she could look to see what was in the bag. Huck replied, "Sure" and handed the bag to her. She unzipped the bag about half way and looked into it. She let out a scream and dropped the bag. About two dozen small snakes wiggled out of the bag onto the floor of the plane. Panic set in immediately. Passengers started getting out of their seats and running toward the rear of the plane. The shifting of the weight in the plane caused it to be unstable. The captain of the plane told the co-pilot to take over so he could determine what was going on the passenger compartment. When he came through the door of the cockpit, he saw chaos. Some passengers were sitting on the tops of their seats, many others had run to the back of the plane and one elderly lady was trying to hit Huck. The flight attendant told the captain that Huck's bag had been full of snakes which were all on the floor of the plane. The pilot asked Huck, "What kind of snakes were in the bag?" Huck replied, "Mostly grass snakes, three or four rat snakes and a couple of baby rattlers."

A barrier was put up at the bulkhead to keep the snakes from crawling toward the back of the plane. The pilot took Huck to the cockpit for his protection from several very hostile passengers. The pilot skillfully flew the tail heavy plane to the airport and landed it safely. Passengers left the plane from the rear via an inflated slide. After the passengers were all out of the plane, the pilot took Huck back into the cabin, handed him his bag and said, "Gather up every single snake." About thirty minutes later, Huck reported that he had all of the snakes back in the bag. Security guards escorted him off of the plane and turned him over to his very embarrassed father. I have often wondered whether Huck's story had created the impetus for the movie "Snakes on a Plane" which came out in 2006.

A Girl in Every Port

My client was an airline pilot who had been served by his wife with divorce papers. I had filed an answer to a divorce petition filed by my airline pilot's wife, after he was served with papers. He had told me that the case would be uncomplicated due to agreements reached with his wife. The next week I received a set of interrogatories. Interrogatories are questions which have to be answered in writing. I forwarded the questions to my client so that he could give me his response to the questions. One of the interrogatories asked the question.

"If you have had sexual relations with anyone other than your spouse during your marriage, state the name, address and telephone number of the person or persons and state the location and date of each incident."

My client called upon receipt of the interrogatories. "Do I really have to answer the sex question?" he asked. "Yes," I responded. In a panic stricken voice he pleaded, "Could I possibly come see you right now?" I agreed to stay late to talk to him. He arrived very quickly after we had spoken. He never sat down in my office. He was pacing the floor while he tried to explain the breadth of the potential problem. He showed me a black address book with listings of all of the cities he flew in and out of over the years. There must have been thirty cities listed in his book. Under each city listed there were three or more names, addresses and phone numbers of women. He explained that he had not slept alone in years. He would call ahead and arrange for sleeping accommodations with one of the women living near his flight's destination. He had the ladies ranked by number and would start by calling his first choice and working down the list. He told me that if all else failed, he would shack up with one of the flight attendants. "Just settle the case," he pleaded. "I cannot afford the buses it would take to bring all the ladies to the courthouse."

In retrospect, it was not a complicated case. His wife got everything she wanted. He did not have to answer the "sex question" and he never went to court. He sent several pilots to me over the years. I should have sent him to a good sex therapist.

A Flight to California

The trip was part business and part vacation. I had co-authored a book with Bill Dorsaneo and Jo Lynne Merrill titled "Texas Family Law Trial Guide." My publisher, Matthew-Bender, had an office in San Francisco, California. I met with the editor of the book at least every other year. It was hardly a burden to travel to northern California for a short business meeting and then spend the rest of the week enjoying the area surrounding San Francisco. The flight from Dallas to San Francisco was usually a pleasant one. My wife liked window seats and I preferred aisle seats on the right side of the plane when facing the front so I could stretch out my bad left leg. Most of the time, no one sat in the middle seat between us. This flight was the exception.

After we were seated, one of the flight attendants brought a young girl to our row. She was flying unaccompanied to spend time with her father who lived in California. After she was seated in the middle seat and had her seat belt fastened, she turned to Ann, and asked, "Are you here to take care of me?" Ann responded, "It sure looks like it." That was the start of a wonderful flight. Emily was a precocious six year old. She was full of questions. She wanted to know everything about both of us. She volunteered information about herself, her mom and her dad. After the in-flight meal was served, she looked at me and said, "You will need to cut my meat for me." You can tell from the fact that there was an in-flight meal that this incident took place some time ago. After the meal, she announced that she was sleepy and would like to take a nap. She looked around quizzically and commented to Ann, "There's really not enough room unless I put my head in your lap." Ann folded up the arm rest between the seats and put a pillow in her lap. Emily put her head on the pillow and was asleep immediately. When the plane started its descent, Emily woke up.

After we had landed and taxied to the gate, the flight attendant came to get Emily to escort her to meet her father. Emily told the flight attendant that her new friends would be going with her to meet Daddy. The first class passengers had deplaned. We left the plane with the flight attendant holding Emily's left hand and I was holding her right hand. As we approached Emily's father, she excitedly stated, "Daddy, daddy, I want you to meet my lawyer." Ann and I introduced ourselves to her father and told him what a delightful daughter he had. I have always hoped that I would get a chance to meet another Emily on a flight going somewhere. She was one of the highlights of the trip.

I Can't Give Up My Cigarettes

I was shocked when the prospective client was shown into my office. She was not just pretty, she was movie star gorgeous. I started the interview by asking, "How can I help you?" She smiled and said, "I need a divorce." "Why do you need a divorce?" I asked. Her response totally dumbfounded me. "My husband will not make love to me," she replied. I later learned that she had finished second in one of the biggest beauty pageants in the country. "That stretches my imagination to the point of confusion," I answered. Why any man would not want to make love to a lady as beautiful as you, I thought to myself. "Why doesn't he want to make love to you?" I asked. "I've burned him real bad a couple of times" she replied in a low voice. "I do not understand, what do you mean?"

The explanation which followed was and still is the strangest reason anyone has given me for wanting a divorce. She explained, "I know this sounds weird, but I have never been able to achieve satisfaction during sex, you know, have a climax, unless I was smoking a cigarette while I was having sex. I've burned him real bad on the neck a couple of times. He told me that unless I stopped smoking while we were having sex that he would not make love to me anymore. I just can't give up my cigarettes."

I tried to get her to consider getting him an asbestos collar, but she wouldn't listen. The couple was divorced shortly thereafter. Two years later, I received a wedding invitation from her. She was marrying a gentleman who owned a nudist camp northwest of Denton, Texas. My wife vetoed our attending. About a year later, I received a postcard, which was inside an envelope. My former client was wearing nothing but a banner, over one shoulder and between her breasts, proclaiming she was "Mrs. Nude Texas."

Happy Birthday Moses

I was impressed when I saw the name of the prospective client. It was a prominent Dallas surname. The lady who came to see me was also impressive. She was tall, blonde and beautiful. She was involved in a divorce not of her choosing. Her husband had gone to a high school reunion and encountered his high school sweetheart. His marriage to my client was not without problems. They had a beautiful young daughter and all of the material things that everyone assumes would eliminate any problems which might arise. Unfortunately, that is not the way things work. The husband was very angry about how my client spent his money which was not community property. The court in Texas can divide community property which has been acquired other than by gift, devise or inheritance or owned prior to the marriage. The law does not allow the judge to award one party's separate property to the other party. One might say that my client was a bit spoiled and accustomed spending money however she wanted, irrespective of whether it was his separate property or community. The husband's attorney and I had known each other a long time and we were able to agree that my client would continue to reside in the community residence while the case was going on.

I received calls from my client often and she was what attorneys called a "High Maintenance Client." She called one morning to invite me and my wife to a birthday party she was giving for a friend. I explained that I did not socialize with clients while their cases were pending. She said, "You should make an exception; the birthday party is for Charlton Heston." I was sorely tempted and told her I appreciated the invitation, but did not think it was a good idea for me to attend. Little did I know that I would be involved in the party whether I wanted to be or not. The fact that she spent over forty thousand dollars on the party did not go over well with her husband or his attorney. The party was held on one of the most prestigious streets in the Park Cities. Caterers, florists, party planners and a band were all part of the extravaganza. The house had a large deck on the back of the second floor of the house which overlooked the pool, putting green and expansive back yard. Unfortunately, my client selected the second floor deck as the venue for the band.

I was getting ready for bed while listening to the ten o'clock news when the phone rang. It was my client, who was in a state of panic. She excitedly explained that someone had called the police because the band was too loud. She expected me to tell her what to do. Not having had any wine that evening, my mind was fairly alert. I told her to tell the band to start packing up immediately, but not to leave until she had executed the second part of the plan. I reminded her that Mr. Heston was the president of the National Rifle Association. I suggested that she take him to the study which was on far west side of the house. The band was on the deck at the far-east end of the house. I told her that when the police arrived she should take them immediately into the study to meet Mr. Heston. I assured her that one or more the policemen were probably members of the NRA and even if they weren't, they all would want to meet Moses from the movie The Ten Commandments. I told her that as soon as the policemen were in the study, someone acting on her behalf should get the band into their van and out of the Park Cities. She promised that she would follow my instructions and call me and let me know how things had worked.

About 10:45 p.m., the phone rang again. She was ecstatic. "It worked great," she proclaimed. The policemen loved talking to Mr. Heston and by the time they were finished visiting, the band had been gone for fifteen minutes. They thanked her for being able to meet Mr. Heston and commented that they had no idea why someone would have complained about noise that they never heard. I was pleased that my advice had helped avoid what my client thought would be a very embarrassing situation. However, it would not be the last problem I would have to solve.

The settlement of the case took a good while due to the complexity of the property issues. The settlement included a schedule for my client moving out of the residence and the husband taking possession. An inspection of the property to determine whether it was in good condition was a required in order for my client receiving a very substantial check for her interest in the property. The balance due on my fee was to be paid from funds received from the check my client was to receive. I was not going to take any chances of the condition of the house being unacceptable to the husband or his attorney. I sent two "Merry Maids" to the house for three days prior to the inspection. The house was so clean that it squeaked. The husband and his attorney were lavish in their praise of the condition of the house. I was ready to get the check and leave when the husband said, "I want to look at the garage." The garage was larger than my house. It could hold four or five cars and had a kitchen and living room on the ground level. The second floor had four bedrooms and a number of storage rooms. I had not even thought about checking out the garage. You could not see the garage from the back of the house because a row of huge photinia bushes lined the driveway almost all the way to the garage and blocked the view. The driveway leading to the garage was along the west border of the lot.

We turned north down the driveway and walked toward the huge garage. As we came around the corner, past the photinias, my heart sank. There in the center of the garage, eight feet off of the ground, was a sign which read, "ASSHOLE'S GARAGE." The husband turned bright red. He glared at me and screamed, "Not only are you not going to get the check, you are not going to get a #$&%*! Nickel until that sign comes down." I told him that if I had known about the sign, it would have been taken down before the inspection.

I asked him if I could borrow a ladder and a screwdriver so I could take down the sign. He answered angrily, "I didn't help put it up and I am not going to help you take it down."

It was a warm summer day. I was wearing a conservative navy suit, white shirt and striped tie. I told the attorney and husband that I would be back as soon as I could get the tools to take down the sign. I was told that if that was very long, they might be gone. I went out to the street in front of the house and looked up and down the block. Eureka! There was an electrician's truck in a former client's driveway across the street and about five houses down. I took off my coat and tie and hustled down the street. Fortunately, my client was home. I explained to him and the electrician what had happened. They were both laughing about my dilemma. I had to promise to bring the sign for them to see in order to get a ladder and a very large screwdriver. I hurried back to the house, hoping that the husband

and his attorney would still be there. They were still there and to add insult to injury, they wanted to watch me take down the sign. I positioned the ladder to give me the best leverage with the screwdriver. I have always had really strong hands and forearms. I put the screwdriver into the slot of the screw and tried to turn it to the left to loosen the screw. Nothing, absolutely nothing happened. I changed my position so that I could grip the screwdriver with both hands. After straining greatly, I finally felt a little movement. I was sweating buckets and the one screw I was working on had moved less than one-half inch. I crawled down off of the ladder, took off my dress shirt and my undershirt. They took mercy on me and let me get a drink of water. Back up the ladder I went with my undershirt wrapped around the handle of the screwdriver to get a better grip. When I finally got the first screw out of the stud, I looked at it closely. It was a four inch wood screw. By the time I had removed the second screw and taken down the sign, forty-five minutes had elapsed. The sign was not some cheap, handmade sign. It was professionally made and looked much like a street sign you might see. It was slightly longer than three feet. I got the check I'd come for and took it and the sign out to my car. I put back on my dress shirt, hoping not to do too much damage to the back of my car seat. About two minutes after leaving the house, I got a phone call. I answered to hear a giggling voice ask, "Did everybody think the sign was funny?" In no uncertain terms I told my client that no one thought the sign was funny and that in addition to my regular hourly rate, I was charging her $5,000.00 for removing the sign. Her response helped me understand the frustrations of her husband regarding her spending habits. "If you got the check, it's no big deal," she responded. "When can I get my sign back?" she asked. "You can't. The sign now belongs to me" I responded.

I still have the sign in my office.

The Saga of Jerry John Jordan

He was from a wealthy family. Not old money; it was wealth that had been earned through hard work. He and his brother were the beneficiaries of a hard-driving father who offered a service that was needed by many kinds of companies in North Texas. The brothers were as different as night and day. Jerry John was the handsome one. A deep tan and jet black hair and a rugged, swarthy look about him. He drove one of the "hottest" cars of anyone at our high school. I never heard anyone describe him as serious. He was a fun-lover of the first order.

His brother was known to be a serious, intelligent student who was also a good athlete. It wasn't that Jerry John was not intelligent; he just never felt the need to make others think so. Both brothers had good looking, intelligent, popular girlfriends. Jerry John's brother is still married to his high school sweetheart.

Jerry John took a different path. His first marriage was to his high school sweetheart and lasted two years. The second marriage lasted fifteen years or so and produced several children. When I helped Jerry John through his first divorce, I never dreamed that it would be the first of many cases to come. For a period of years, Jerry John sought the company of younger women. His third wife was about fifteen years younger than he was. I don't remember how long that third marriage lasted. I do remember that I hoped that he would do a better job of selecting a fourth wife. Over the next few years, the women got younger as Jerry John got older. I have represented him in six divorces and one annulment. Some of the stories are of love found and lost, and in one case, found, lost, found again and then lost again. They are some of the most unusual cases I have handled over the years.

The greatest coincidence that has ever happened in my years of practice is that all of his cases were in the same court. Each case is assigned by computer into one of the family courts. There were four courts when Jerry John started his travels through the vagaries of matrimony and seven courts at the time of his last divorce. Needless to say, the judge who handled each of his divorces got to know Jerry John very well. The longer you know him, the better you like him. I have his permission to share some of my favorite memories over the fifty plus years of our friendship.

On several occasions, Jerry John had spent a week at my condominium in the Rockies. He loved the place and I was happy for him to go there. I was always pleased when the receptionist announced that Jerry John was on the phone. He started the conversation by asking me, "Would you let me get married in your hot tub up in Colorado?" I knew he was single, having handled his most recent divorce. I told him, "If you can find a preacher who will marry you in the hot tub, go for it." Jerry John had previously been married on horseback. One might say that he is not a conventional thinker or doer. He was able to talk a Unitarian preacher into kneeling beside the hot tub and performing the ceremony. The bride was in her twenties and Jerry John was approaching his fifties. After the ceremony—and I'm not sure how long after— the new bride broke a glass of Jack Daniels over Jerry John's head. After getting sewed up, he called me at home to ask if I could get him an annulment. I was able to get the marriage annulled only to have my favorite client remarry the young lady in a couple of weeks. There must have been magic in the water of the hot tub.

One of my favorite stories is about Jerry John's wife taking a straight razor to one of his custom made saddles. His fourth divorce was pending when his irate spouse sliced up his saddle something fierce. Deep cuts had removed most of the sterling silver trim off of the saddle. One stirrup was cut off entirely. The rest of the saddle had deep gashes over the seat and the saddle horn. He called to ask if there was something we could about her destruction of his favorite saddle. I filed a motion for contempt and asked that she be put in jail and have to pay for the damage to the saddle.

Jerry John brought the saddle to the office and I carried it to court over my shoulder. When we got to court, I put the saddle down on the jury rail, which is the low wall that separates where the jury would sit in a trial from the area where the attorneys sit. There was no jury, but the rail was the most visible place for the saddle to sit during the proceedings. The judge, who had grown to like Jerry John over the years, was not sympathetic to the wife. The wife was ordered to bring $3,500.00 to the court before 4:00 P.M. to pay for the saddle or spend three days in jail. The judge gave her one phone call to try to raise the money. About fifteen minutes before four, several friends and family members showed up with the cash to pay for the saddle. It was counted out and turned over to Jerry John.

The judge told his wife she could leave the courtroom. The lady had steam coming out of her ears. Her face was bright red and she was breathing heavily. As she was leaving the courtroom, the bailiff called out to her, "Ma'am, you forgot your saddle." The wife turned and screamed, "F--- both of you." The bailiff turned and asked Jerry John, "If she doesn't want the saddle, can I have it?" "It's yours," responded Jerry John.

The next divorce was the most memorable of all. The attorney for the next wife was an aggressive young lawyer who thought he was going to get a pound of flesh from Jerry John. He thought he was going to be able to show that Jerry John was spending money on totally inappropriate things. He was saying disparaging things about Jerry John, accusing him of being a thief and a philanderer.

He suggested that Jerry John had bought one of his former wives a new car during the pendency of the current divorce. After a few more caustic statements about Jerry John, the Judge hammered down her gavel and stated, "I have known Mr. Jordan for many years and I do not want to hear any more comments about his character. My experience is that he is a generous and kind person." She then looked to Jerry John and asked," Did you buy your former wife a car?" "Yes your honor, I did" he answered. "Why did you do that?" queried the judge. "I got a call from my second wife. She told me that she was driving down Central Expressway and the transmission in her car fell out on the road. She got over to the shoulder, stopped and called me. She explained that our grandbabies were in the car with her when the transmission dropped out on the road. I asked her if blue was still her favorite color. She said it was, so I sent a new Chevrolet over to her house that afternoon. I wasn't going to let our grandbabies ride around in an unsafe car."

The judge looked disgustedly at my opposing counsel and asked, "Now just what's wrong with that?" The ruling in the case was very fair to Jerry John.

The last time I went to court with Jerry John was to handle the adoption of his sixth wife's nine year old daughter. His second wife and his last wife were the best two of the lot. We had terminated the little girl's father's rights as a result of his abandonment and non-support of his daughter. After having been married to her mother for over a year, Jerry John wanted to adopt his stepdaughter. The case was assigned to a different court than the one where the divorces had occurred. I went to the judge of the assigned court and explained about the six divorces. I asked if she would transfer the adoption to the court of the judge who had heard all of the divorces. She agreed. As I said earlier, the judge had heard all of the divorces had grown fond of Jerry John. She was flattered that he had wanted her to hear the adoption. After the adoption hearing, the judge congratulated Jerry John, his wife and his newly adopted daughter. A picture was taken of the four of them. The judge then asked the wife and daughter if they could wait in the hall, while she talked to Jerry John for a minute. After they were out of the courtroom, the judge looked straight at Jerry John, shook her finger at him and said, "I never want to see you in my court again." He hugged the judge and said, "I have no intention of ever needing you again." The last time I called Jerry John, a young lady answered the phone. She explained that her mom and Jerry John were out of town. She told me that she would be graduating from college in the spring and she still remembered the day she was adopted.

LAW SCHOOL FINISHING THE PROCESS

The Third Year

It was in the fall of 1968 when I started my last year of law school. I had taken almost all of the required courses and was going to take some courses which sounded interesting to me. I took Labor Law, a seminar in Legal Ethics taught by Joe McKnight, Science Technology and the Law, Oil and Gas, Income Taxation, Marital Property, and Secured Transactions which was taught by the Dean. I was also in charge of the Moot Court competition.

The fall semester had one of the unforgettable events of my law school career. The Student Bar Association annually sponsored a contest called "Miss Carriage of Justice." For several years the law students had felt that the girls being sent to participate by the undergraduate sororities were not as pretty as they should have been. Some of my classmates knew the most well-known stripper in Dallas, a young lady who went by the name, Bubbles Cash. Bubbles was very well endowed, whether by Mother Nature or some talented plastic surgeon. She had appeared at several Dallas Cowboy football games and caused quite a commotion.

We entered Bubbles in the Miss Carriage of Justice Competition under her real name, as a representative of one of girl's dormitories. The vote was rigged. Bubbles won by a landslide. The crowning of the winner was scheduled to occur at the annual touch football game between two of the legal fraternities. The Dean was scheduled to attend as was our professor who socialized with the students. Professor Charmatz was only about five foot six inches tall. Bubbles showed up in a mini-shirt that left very little to one's imagination.

Her blouse was even more revealing. The Dean looked like he was going to have a stroke. The Professor who would be presenting the bouquet of roses and the crown to Bubbles had a grin on his face from ear to ear. Bubbles accepted the crown and the roses and then pulled the professors face between her ample breasts. The Dean was not happy. Neither were the nominees sent by the sororities.

Exams were over and I was looking forward to the Christmas holidays when my plans were derailed. I had experienced nausea and lower back pains for a number of years. None of my doctors had ever been able to figure out what was causing the problem. My internist in Dallas told me that the next time I had the problem I was to call him and he would meet me in the emergency room at Methodist Hospital in Oak Cliff. I made that fateful call on Christmas Eve. My wife had strep throat and so I drove myself to the hospital. My doctor, Arvel Haley, was the father of four sons who were all friends of mine. Now they are all doctors. Dr. Haley did a number of tests and discovered that I had a congenitally deformed right kidney which did not drain properly. Dr. Haley lined up Dr. Ted Boone, a great surgeon, for the reconstructive surgery which was scheduled for December 26, 1968. The ureter on my right kidney was about two-thirds of the way up the side of the kidney instead of being at the bottom quadrant. As a result, the kidney couldn't drain properly and there were fourteen stones collected in the bottom of my kidney. The surgery relocated my ureter, removed the stones and hooked up an outside drain so that I could wear a cute little bag which would collect urine. I spent most of the post-Christmas holidays in Methodist Hospital. Chuck Chapman, a fraternity brother and law school classmate and I watched SMU beat Oklahoma in the Bluebonnet Bowl on December 28, 1968. My dear wife had strep throat and could not visit me in hospital. For the first four weeks of the second semester, I had to wear my collection bag on my belt. The repaired kidney was functioning at about 20% of normal before the surgery and is now still functioning at better than 80% of normal.

The Last Semester

The final semester of law school is the easiest unless you are fighting to be in the top ten percent of the class. Many of the top firms will not interview you for a job if you are not in the top ten percent. I had decided after the first year that I did not want to work hard enough to try to be near the top of the class. I remember one of my classmates saying the top ten percent would be working for him in five years. I had also decided that I did not want to work in a large firm. I don't think in retrospect that I was rationalizing because I had no chance to work for one of the big firms. I never have been able to function in an atmosphere where being politically correct was the required course of action. I was introduced to an older attorney by a longtime friend. The gentleman had been corporate counsel to a company which had become one of the Fortune 500. Before that he had worked with a labor union. After his retirement as corporate counsel, he had started handling family law cases and serving as an arbitrator. I had really enjoyed my family law classes and also found labor law to be fascinating. He also continued to represent the family of the founder of the corporation for which he had been corporate counsel. I went to work for him as a law clerk in the spring semester of my last year.

I became a family lawyer by accident. I graduated from law school in spring, 1969 and was scheduled to take the bar examination. The Family Code was passed by the Texas legislature that spring and was to become law on January 1, 1970. The terminology used in family law in Texas was about to change dramatically. The

Family Code was an attempt to take Texas family law into the twentieth century. The drafters were forward thinking idealists who wanted to create a kinder and gentler way of dealing with divorce, child custody and juvenile delinquency. Title One of the Family Code, "Husband and Wife," was passed during my last semester of school and became effective January 1, 1970. Title Two was named "Parent and Child" and became effective on January 1, 1974. Title Three, "Children in Need of Supervision" became effective on September 1, 1973.

I asked my boss if he would like for me to take the new statutes and revise all of the divorce forms the firm used so that on January 1, 1970 he would not have to reinvent the wheel. He replied that he thought that would be a good idea.

The prevailing procedure in the late '60's and early 70's for the creation of divorce pleadings was for the attorney to call his secretary into the office and dictate the text. I reviewed the intake forms for new divorce clients and saw no logical connection between the acquisition of information and how the information was put down on paper to be filed with the court. The system was fraught with possibilities for errors due to the mistakes made in dictation and the absence of any logical order in which information was acquired. There was no quality control. Documents were typed with either three or four carbon copies. Correcting mistakes was a time-consuming and messy process which resulted in documents that looked unprofessional.

I decided that these methods were all wrong. When I was working on this project, there were no computers. I started gathering the documents found in Stayton's Forms and Texas Jurisprudence Forms. I reviewed a number of petitions for divorce which my boss had filed for clients. My goal was to create a methodology whereby documents could be produced without any spoken words by the attorney to the secretary.

I decided to create a check list which would allow the attorney to take down the information needed to prepare a divorce petition in exactly the same order it would appear in the document to be filed with the court. In the check list, the attorney would include information such as the person's name, address, and any children of the marriage. Then he would simply circle numbers and letters which would correspond to forms containing the same numbers and letters. I really got excited about how I thought I could significantly change how documents were created and at the same time improve the quality of the product. I spent a tremendous amount of time during the spring and early summer of 1969 working on my check lists and forms.

In retrospect, my decision not to take a formal bar examination review course was really brash and foolish. Naïvely, I thought that since I had gone to law school for three years, there was no reason to waste time taking a review course. I did not think about the questions which might be asked from subjects I had never studied. Fortunately, I passed the bar exam on my first try. During the time I should have been taking the bar review, I was polishing and re-polishing my check lists and forms. When I had finished the project, I took it to my boss and explained how the system would work. His reaction shocked me. He looked at the check lists and forms and asked a few questions. Then he exclaimed, "This is too good to keep to ourselves. We should give it to the State Bar of Texas." He called Bar headquarters and offered the form book to them for publication. Gene Cavin was the representative who agreed to publish the first form book ever issued by the State Bar of Texas.

Although I had written every form and questionnaire in the original book, the State Bar decided that to list me, a recent law graduate who was not licensed to practice, as the author would not help create credibility or sales. I did get mention as a contributor along with notable professors and attorneys who did little or nothing to create "Forms for Divorce and Annulment under the Family Code."

I took the bar examination in June. Until I found out whether or not I had passed the bar, I was a law school graduate who was not a licensed attorney. My wife and I took the longest vacation of our fifty-year marriage and spent three weeks in Europe. Her father was born in London and had cousins there whom we met for the first time. We visited England, Germany, Austria and Italy before we returned to the U.S. We were in Vienna when the Eagle landed on the moon. When we returned, I learned that I had passed the bar.

My boss was Jack Johannes. He had graduated from law school during the "Great Depression." He took on work for no compensation with the hope that he would impress someone who would hire him in the future. A man named Elmer Doolin asked Jack to help him with his struggling new company named Frito. Jack became corporate counsel and vice-president for development. He retired after the merger with Lay's Potato Chips. At age sixty-five, Jack became a family lawyer and shortly thereafter, so did I.

I memorize and remember things very easily. After finishing work on the form book, I realized that I could recite Title One of the Family Code verbatim. Attorneys and Judges started calling me to ask questions about the new code after it became law. Shortly after the law became effective, I asked my father, "What should I do? Almost everyone thinks I know everything about the new law and I have never handled a divorce case." He responded, "Don't tell a soul; they will never figure out that you don't know everything."

I decided to create a plan to become a good family lawyer. My sweet grandmother Giltner had a talk with me about success before I started practicing law. She asked me, "Do you know why 95% percent of the people never achieve their goals?" Without waiting for me to respond, she explained, "They never take the time to write down where they are going, so they never know when or if they get there." She explained that you need to have short-term, medium-term and long-term goals, but they must be written down. You also need to write down your plan for how you intend to achieve each goal.

"The Law West of the Trinity"

Oak Cliff had the distinction of having a Justice of the Peace who was known as "The Law West of the Trinity." Justice of the Peace, Bill Richburg, ruled Oak Cliff like a feudal lord. He was a very powerful influence on life in Oak Cliff. By the time I got to law school, the city of Dallas had built a courthouse on South Beckley in Oak Cliff. Judge Richburg did not have a law degree, which is not required in Texas to be a Justice of the Peace. He did have excellent judgment, intelligence and a sense of fairness that far exceeded many of the law-degreed judges who were elected by the public.

During my time in law school, I became frustrated that the faculty did not think it was important to teach the students how to be lawyers. After I was elected to the Student Bar Association, I lobbied to be the student representative to the faculty curriculum committee. I succeeded in becoming the student liaison. I was told by the professor who was the head of the committee that the goal of the law school was "to teach the students how to *think* like lawyers." He volunteered to me that the job of teaching students how to *be* lawyers was left to the downtown law firms. He acknowledged that less than 15% of the class would be hired by those downtown law firms. Very few practice courses were available to SMU law students during the mid to late sixties. Legal clinic, land use planning and tax planning courses were the extent of the practical courses in the curriculum. The philosophy at other law schools, such as Baylor, was much more oriented toward teaching their students what lawyers needed to know to competently represent clients. I decided to do something to correct what I thought was a big hole in our legal education.

I called Justice of the Peace, Bill Richburg. I proposed that we create a mutually beneficial program that would help him handle his huge Saturday docket and give law students the opportunity to be lawyers. The students would interview clients and present their cases to the Judge in an orderly and organized fashion. Judge Richburg was excited about the idea and welcomed the opportunity to work with law students. The Judge would assign a law student to assist each party to a case. The law student would have fifteen minutes to talk to his client, identify issues and determine requested relief. When the case was called by the Judge, the law student would succinctly state the issues and the requested relief.

There were six to eight law students who traveled to Oak Cliff each Saturday to work in the Oak Cliff Justice Court. The time I spent working to help Judge Richburg on Saturdays taught me more about interviewing and presenting my client's position than anything I learned at law school. I never asked permission to create the program or to participate in it. I am sure that the mentality of the faculty curriculum committee would have prevailed and we would have been told we could not volunteer our services to the Justice Court. Not to share some of our cases in the Justice Court would be to deny you the opportunity to understand how justice works in the courts closest to the vast majority of our citizens.

Judge Bill Richburg was tough but fair. However some of his practices would have never passed muster with the American Civil Liberties Union. Judge Richburg had a dictating machine on his bench, next to the witness chair. It was a DeJur Grundig Stenorette. The unit was rectangular in shape and about twelve inches by ten inches. It stood about two inches high at the front and three inches high at the back. There was a light on the face of the machine which lit up in a red color when the operator pushed a button on the hand-held control device to record. There was a cord that connected the unit to the microphone.

Judge Richburg would tell parties to the disputes who were testifying that the machine was a lie detector. He would make the witness put his hand on top of the machine while he testified and would hold the control device out of sight of the witness. If at any time he thought the witness was not being truthful, he would push the button on the hand-held control unit and the red light would come on. He would look at the red light, look at the witness and say, "It looks like you are being untruthful; let's start this over." He might cause the light to come on several times during the testimony of a single witness. Invariably the witness would level with the Judge.

Judge Richburg had the courage and common sense to deal with a problem that the elected judges, who were attorneys, ignored. Many attorneys and almost all of the judges treated Justices of the Peace the way medical doctors treated chiropractors. Texas did not then and does not now recognize same-sex relationships in the way the law deals with married couples. Same-sex couples often accumulated property over a period of years which needed to be divided if the relationship ended. On the few occasions when such actions were filed in divorce courts or the district courts, the cases would be quickly thrown out. Judge Richburg would hear these disputes and apply the principles of dividing a partnership. The parties were treated with respect by the only judge in Dallas County who would try to help them resolve their problems.

Of all of the cases I either tried or observed in Judge Richburg's court, three stories stand out in my mind. The first case involved the Boys Baseball coach, for whom I had played when I was twelve. I was assigned to represent the wife in a Peace Bond hearing. Peace Bonds can be granted upon request when one person is doing something to threaten the peace or well-being of another individual. Peace Bond hearings probably took up at least half of the Judge's time. When I saw the man my client was complaining about, I recognized him as my baseball coach. I asked my classmate to switch clients so I could represent my old coach. The classmate agreed. After interviewing my client, I learned that he and his wife had recently been divorced. After the divorce, he had received a call at work from a neighbor informing him that his ex-wife had a moving truck at the house and was removing the contents. He had been awarded the house in the divorce. So he rushed home, went down the alley and entered the house through the back door. As he went toward the front of the house, he saw his former wife, preparing to go out of the front door with an arm load of items he had been awarded by the judge. He followed her and as she started down the front steps, he kicked her in the fanny. She then filed suit requesting a Peace Bond. Upon further questioning, my client acknowledged that neither he nor his wife had been pleased with the divorce Judge's division of the property. He explained that he had been awarded the washer and dryer and she had been awarded the window air conditioners. He said he didn't care about the washer and dryer, but really wanted the air conditioners. I went to my classmate and proposed that his client get the washer and dryer, my client get the window air conditioners and that she dismiss the request for the Peace Bond. He consulted with his client and said, "You've got it." This case exemplifies how we were able to help clear the docket and also gain invaluable experience in helping clients that we would never have learned at our law school.

The next case represents what you may consider the dark side. The wife filed a request for a Peace Bond to prohibit her husband from having sex with their neighbor's horse. After swearing to tell the truth and having his hand placed upon the "lie detector," the husband admitted to having had more than a six-pack of "My Budweiser." He explained to the Judge that he had gotten really drunk before he had committed the act of which he had been accused. Judge Richburg granted the Peace Bond and also set a "Horse Courting Bond." He explained to the husband that if he was ever caught fooling around with the neighbor's horse or any other horse, he would be placed in jail for ten years and would have to post a $10,000.00 bond which would be forfeited to his wife.

It was not uncommon for Judge Richburg to grant "Drinking Bonds." On one occasion a wife had filed a request for a Peace Bond because her husband drank excessively and roughed her up when he was drunk. The judge listened intently, looked directly at the husband, picked up the phone and said, "Sheriff, this is Judge Richburg. How quick can you get a deputy down here to pick up a wife beater? Ten minutes? I will call you right back." Judge Richburg looked at the husband and said, "I'm going to grant the Peace Bond and set a $5,000.00 Drinking Bond. If you get caught getting drunk again and mistreating your wife, your bond will be forfeited and you will go to jail for five years." The husband was in shock. He asked the Judge if he had a choice. "What do you mean?" asked Judge Richburg. The husband responded, "Could I just give up my wife and keep on drinking my beer?" Judge Richburg reached for the phone and said, "Sheriff, send someone down here to pick up a worthless wife beater."

On occasion, Judge Richburg would make a very punitive ruling on the first case of the day. He would often tell the bailiff to keep the person who received the rough treatment in the courtroom. The rest of the docket was often resolved with many agreements between the parties. After all the cases had been handled, Judge Richburg would have the bailiff bring back the person whose case had been heard first. Judge Richburg would look at the person and say, "You are really lucky. I feel like I might have been a little tough on you earlier this morning." He would then modify his ruling.

Several years later, I had the opportunity to thank Judge Richburg in a way he never expected. I was Chairman of the Family Law Section of the Dallas Bar in 1973-74. One of the enjoyable parts of being chairman was the responsibility of obtaining speakers for our monthly meetings. One of the first speakers I invited was Judge Richburg. When I invited him to speak on "Family Law as Practiced in the Justice of the Peace Court" I thought he was going to cry. He accepted my invitation and told me he had never been in the Bar Association headquarters—let alone been asked to speak to some of its members.

His presentation was attended by the largest

group of attorneys who had ever attended a monthly meeting. He did a wonderful job of educating us and entertaining us at the same time.

Retirement

Prior to graduation from law school, I had to report to Carswell Air Force Base in Fort Worth, Texas for a physical exam. I anticipated being called back to active duty to serve a little less than two years in JAG, the Judge Advocate General Corps of the Air Force. I reported for my physical and was checked from stem to stern. The doctors were very interested in the kidney surgery which had occurred about two months before. My medical records showed that in my time on active duty I had gone to the doctor because of lower back pain on my right side and nausea. None of the service doctors had ever been able to diagnose the problem. After the surgery to relocate the ureter and remove the stones, the kidney was functioning with about eighty percent efficiency. But several weeks after the examination, I was notified that I was not going to go back to active duty; instead, I would be medically retired.

According to their evaluation, my knee had not improved and the kidney problem had been ruled to be a "service connected condition." The combination of the two medical problems meant that I was rated as having a thirty percent disability. The decision didn't make any sense to me. I knew that my knee was still a problem, but not if I was working as an attorney. The kidney problem was congenital. After the surgery my kidney was working better than ever. The Air Force also added that they had more lawyers than they needed. My orders setting out the conditions of my retirement arrived and gave me the severance date of August 6, 1966. I had become one of the few retired first lieutenants in Air Force history.

I decided that when I graduated from law school I would help veterans who could not afford legal assistance. Upon receiving my law license I notified the Veterans Administration of my willingness to help. About that time I received my first "retirement check."

I was sent thirty percent of my basic pay as a first lieutenant. The check was for about one hundred dollars. I sent the check back to the return address on the envelope. I did the same thing with the second check. I felt that I had been adequately compensated because my legal education was paid for by vocational rehabilitation. Several weeks after I sent back the second check, I received a call from an officer who identified himself as the General in charge of all military retirement pay. He said, "I don't know why you are sending back the retirement checks. I really don't care why you are doing it, but I want it to stop immediately." "No one has ever sent back a check before. If you don't need the money or don't want the money, then give it away to a charity or to anyone else you want. I am having the two checks sent back to you. You will be in more trouble than you can handle if I ever hear that you have sent back another check." I replied simply, "I understand, Sir." I used the checks to help send three underprivileged young people to college, and for other things, but I have never returned another check.

Going to Court

I was back from our post-graduation vacation, working in the law office and waiting for the results of the bar exam. My boss knew someone who knew Mr. Garson Jackson, the clerk of the Texas Supreme Court. The Supreme Court supervises the bar examination and Mr. Jackson was responsible for releasing the results for publication. Somehow I got his private phone number, called him, and asked if I had passed the bar exam. He sputtered a few times, looked at his list and said, "Yes, you passed." Now all I had to do was wait several days for the list to be published. I also found out that John Daniel, a classmate had passed.

It was traditional for the candidates who had passed the exam to go to Austin to be sworn in. John's father was a good friend of a district judge who had indicated it would be an honor to swear in John. I was able to tag along and get sworn in with him. We decided to jump the gun and have Judge Charles Long swear us in several days before the big group. On September 15, 1969, we became licensed attorneys, eligible to practice law in Texas courts.

My first trip to court was to handle a divorce for my boss' maid. The petition for divorce had been filed and service was by publication. It is necessary to officially notify a person when a suit has been filed against them. There are several options. If the suit is "agreed" to as in a divorce when both parties want a divorce to be granted, the non-filing party can execute a waiver of service of process which eliminates the need for the papers to be served. If a waiver is not executed and filed with the court, papers must be served by a sheriff, constable or private process server. The last alternative allows publication of the notice by posting or by having it printed in the locally approved legal newspaper. In order to be entitled to use publication, you have to swear that you do not know where the person is located and that you have made legitimate efforts to locate the person.

I was given a divorce decree and told to meet my client at the courthouse. She was a pleasant lady who had worked for my boss for a long time. I was told that she and her husband had been separated for several years. To "prove up" a divorce it is necessary to ask questions which establish the client's entitlement to be divorced. You must establish that the client has lived in Texas for six months and in the county in which the case was filed for ninety days prior to the filing of the suit. After establishing the basis for residence and domicile, you must show how the respondent was notified of the existence of the suit for divorce. When publication has been used, you have to establish that your client does not know the whereabouts of the respondent. The "prove up" was going smoothly until I asked my client, "How long has it been since you have seen your husband?" She smiled and said, "We slept together last night."

The Judge, who knew I had just been licensed, handed the court file back to me and said, "Come back when you get this in proper order." On my walk back to the office I recalled a quote attributed to Winston Churchill. He said, "Failure is not fatal; it is the courage to continue that counts." But to fail on my first try to handle an uncontested matter still bothers me.

I learned very quickly that anytime there was a chance that the attorney was going to get the proverbial "pie in the face," my boss sent me to court. He told me that I should win half of my cases because the facts would be on my side. He said I should win another twenty-five percent because I had out-prepared my opposing counsel. He said what would determine whether or not I was a really good attorney would be how many cases I could win when the facts were not on my side and opposing counsel had properly prepared. Those statements provided little or no solace after my first failure.

My first trial was also a miserable experience. I was representing the mother of four in a divorce and custody dispute with her husband. I thought I had done a good job of preparing the case. A number of very favorable witnesses were eager to testify that my client was a great mother. The children all wanted to live with their mother. My strategy was to have my best witness, other than my client, take the stand first. Then I would have several other witnesses and finally end my part of the case with my client. The trial was in early November of 1970. Everything was going great and my client was an excellent witness. When I announced, "No more questions of this witness at this time your honor," opposing counsel started his cross-examination of my client.

It was unexpected and brutal. His first question was, "Are you pregnant with your boyfriend's baby?" My client did not answer either yes or no. She responded, "How did you know?" Things went downhill from there. She admitted that she and her boyfriend had taken the four children to the Galveston, Texas beach for a long weekend. They all stayed in the same room. She got pregnant on the trip with all of the children sleeping in the room with her and her boyfriend.

We lost. My client asked me, "Don't you remember my asking you if it was okay to take the kids to Galveston for a long weekend?" I replied, "I remember that I told you that *you* could take the children, but I didn't even know that you had a boyfriend."

I learned a lot from that case. You can never presume that your client knows anything. I have probably offended a number of clients over the years by giving them instructions which weren't necessary. As my sweet grandmother told me, "Common sense is not very common."

I tend to remember best the lessons learned from mistakes. But over the years, I have often gone to court to observe great lawyers ply their trade. You can learn almost as much from watching skillful direct and cross-examination as you can from your own mistakes. An example that comes to mind is the following cross-examination of the wife by the husband's attorney, the same attorney who argued the amicus position with me in the Young case.

Q.   Ma'am, isn't it true that you husband gave you four diamond rings during your marriage?

A.   Yes

Q.   Ma'am, isn't it true that he gave you three mink coats?

A.   Yes

Q.   Ma'am, isn't it true that he gave you a custom Jaguar Van Den Plas automobile?

A.   Yes

Q.   And Ma'am isn't it true that the only thing you ever gave him during your marriage was syphilis?

A.   Between sobs, she uttered a quiet yes.

For all practical purposes, the case was over. The judge awarded the husband almost all of the property which had been accumulated during the relatively short marriage.

Be wary of any lawyer who tells you he has never lost a case. He is either a liar or someone who has not tried many cases.

HOBBIES OUTSIDE OF MY LAW PRACTICE

If I had been able to make a living teaching school and coaching, that's probably what I would have done. I started coaching and officiating sports while I was in college. My coaching experiences have given me some of my fondest memories and I want to share some of them. Over the years I have coached some great kids. Here are four of my favorite stories.

Basketball, Fort Walton Beach, Florida

In the fall of 1964 I got a call from Fred Pitts, the director of the recreation program for the town of Fort Walton Beach, Florida. I had been in training at Tyndall AFB in Panama City. After completing training as a weapons controller, I was assigned to the 729th Communications and Control Squadron at Eglin AFB, outside of Fort Walton Beach. Fred said he had heard that I was a basketball coach. I told him about my experience as a player and coach. He asked if I would coach a team in the league for 11 and 12 year olds who were not taller than 5'6". He explained that they played with an eight-foot, six-inch-high basket. I have always been opposed to playing with a lowered basket. I thought a smaller ball should have only been for third graders. Fred explained that my team had already been chosen from tryouts, even though they did not have a coach.

I agreed to take on the team and scheduled our first practice. I was very pleased at the talent of some of my players. There were three good players and four others who were very athletic, but ignorant of how to play basketball. I felt great about the first team meeting. The other teams had traditional names like the Knicks, the Lakers, the Bulls and the Celtics. I suggested that we select an unconventional name for our team. We all lived on the beautiful gulf coast of northwest Florida with its salt-white beaches, blue waters and abundant sunshine. We decided to be the "Mongolian Sun Worshipers." Our jerseys had a large yellow sunburst on the front and back.

Before the first week of workouts was over, I got

a call from the father of a boy who was in the same grade as my team members. He explained that Bobby had learning disabilities. He had never been able to play on any of the sports teams because of his problems. He asked if there was any chance that he could be a part of our team. I told him that before I could make a decision, I would need to meet Bobby, have a private workout and then talk to the team. His Dad agreed to bring Bobby to the gym at a time when it would be almost empty. I was waiting when they arrived. Bobby was of average height, with well-tanned skin, a shock of brown hair and a friendly smile. I wanted to see how fast he could run, how quick he was and get an idea about his strength. I was amazed! He was as quick as any boy I had ever coached. He was incredibly strong for his size. He was as fast as anyone on the team. He had no clue about the rules of the game or how to shoot or dribble. If I could figure out how to use his talents, he could contribute. I thanked Bobby and his dad, but would not make a commitment without talking to the team.

At our next practice, I sat the team down in a room in the recreation center to talk about Bobby. I first explained about his dad's phone call and my workout with Bobby. We then had a discussion about whether he would help or hurt the team. Several of the team members who had classes with Bobby expressed doubt that he could help the team because of his learning disabilities. I asked if they thought that having Bobby on the team would help them become more tolerant of people who were different. None of them had even considered how having Bobby on the team could help them be better people. One player was concerned that the mandatory substitution rules would work to the team's disadvantage if Bobby had to play during

"Crunch Time," the last few minutes of the game. I assured the team that I could figure out how to keep that from happening. I had no idea about how to do what I was promising, but knew I would be able to figure it out. I excused myself from the room after asking the team to talk it over with me outside of the room. I asked them to send for me when they had decided what they wanted to do. I am not sure what I would have done if the team had decided not to give Bobby a chance. One of the players came to get me. Don spoke for the team when we got back to the room. "We want to help Bobby and we want to give him a chance to help us," Don explained. My work was cut out for me. Before the next practice, I had to figure out how to use Bobby in a way to help him and our team.

At the same time I was trying to integrate Bobby into the team, I also had to teach basic skills to the players who had never been on a team. It was obvious that Bobby would not be able to grasp concepts of offense or defense. He forgot that you had to dribble in order to move the ball down or around the court. I had to design an offense and defense which functioned with four players. If we had to play four on five, we would be at a serious disadvantage. We would have to run. If we could beat the other team up and down the court, we could score before the other team could set their defense. We would have to play a pressing defense, in order to disrupt the other team's offensive flow. The league had a rule against using a full court press, but we could pick them up right at the midcourt line.

In leagues which had mandatory substitution rules, I have never started my best five players. We started two of the less experienced players who played the point positions in our "Karate Defense." Nothing dirty would be tolerated. No tripping, holding, slugging or other violations were acceptable. I explained that I would be disappointed if the other team was able to move the ball into their offensive end of the court. All of the other teams started their best five players. When the mandatory substitutions occurred, we had a significant advantage. I taught them a half-court zone trap which was made famous by John Wooden, the renowned UCLA coach who was called the, "Wizard of Westwood." Our goal was to blitz our opponents in the first quarter and come out with a ten to twelve point lead. All was going well except I still didn't have a clue about how to use Bobby.

After one of our practices, Glenn, who was our best offensive player, complained to me that Bobby was driving him crazy. When we practiced five on five, Bobby would run all over the court chasing the ball or harassing the player with the ball. Glenn explained that the starters could not get into any kind of rhythm because of Bobby. I immediately realized that Glenn had just told me how to use Bobby to help our team. I experimented in practice with Bobby harassing Glenn or Reid or Don. He drove them to distraction. If Bobby could cause that kind of problem for our best players, he could do the same thing to the other team's star.

To his father's great surprise Bobby not only got to play on the team, he was a starter. Our first game confirmed that the tactic would work. With Bobby and Steve starting, while two of our better players were on the bench, we jumped off to a 12 to 2 first quarter lead.

Both Bobby and Steve were aggressive on defense and drew several fouls apiece. After the second quarter, we led 22 to 6. At halftime, Bobby had four fouls and Steve had three. I had already fulfilled all of the mandatory playing time requirements for my substitute players. Soon after the start of the third quarter, Bobby fouled out of the game. He had done his job in spades. Once or twice he rebounded the ball and not remembered to dribble. The other team's star had scored only 2 of their 6 points.

In the fourth quarter the other team had to make mass substitutions to meet the mandatory playing time requirements. My five best players were on the court and it was time to "kick ass and take names." We set an all-time scoring record in our first game.

The season started well and we sailed through our part of the league play undefeated. Unfortunately, a storm was brewing on the horizon. There was an undefeated team in the other half of the league and we would have to play them for the championship. Their star was a 5'6", 135 pound monster named Wade. He was leading the league in scoring and rebounding. He would grow to 6'8" and weigh 245 when he played power forward for Auburn University. I decided not to change a thing about how we would play in the championship game. At the start of every game, I would take Bobby and point out the other team's best player. My instructions to him never changed. "I want you to follow him everywhere he goes on both ends of the court and NEVER LET HIM GET IN FRONT OF YOU." Bobby was guarding the other team's star on both ends of the court. He might not be able to understand how to run our offense or play team defense, but he could follow my simple instruction.

The championship game started before the largest crowd of the season. The local radio station was in attendance. It was obvious from the start that Wade was really irritated with Bobby. On one occasion he pushed Bobby down and drew a foul. Glenn and Reid were running and shooting like never before. We led at halftime by 24 to 8. When the buzzer sounded to end the second quarter, the boys rushed to get a drink at the water fountains in the hall. A minute or so later, Bobby came running up to me with blood covering his nose, face and jersey. I excitedly asked him, "What happened?" Through his tears he explained, "Wade wanted a drink and I WOULD NOT LET HIM GET IN FRONT OF ME. Then he hit me in the face." I hugged him and took him to the bathroom where I washed the blood from his face. I told him, "You did a great job Bobby."

We easily won the game and the city championship. Our team was advancing to the regional championships in Pensacola, Florida. I had the right to add two players to my squad for the playoffs. I chose Wade and another boy named Sherrill to fill out the team.

Later I received a call from the mayor of Fort Walton. He congratulated me on our fine season and then told me that the city council had decided to buy us new uniforms and shoes *if* we would go to the playoffs as the "Fort Walton Beach All-Stars." Our team had a good laugh about the politicians not wanting to be represented by the Mongolian Sun Worshipers. We accepted their offer. We won the regional championship the right to play in the state tournament.

The state tournament was played in Deland, Florida. We drove down to Deland in several cars. My wife and I had three players in my car with us. Reservations had been made for us to stay in a hotel which was close to the gym where we would play. As we approached the hotel, Ann exclaimed, "Did you see that sign?" It said 'Transients Welcome." The rooms were almost clean. You needed a ladder to climb into the bathtub, which you would not want to get into anyway. The kids thought the place was great.

The next morning after breakfast, we went over for a short workout before our early afternoon game. The minute I saw the court I knew we were in trouble. The recreation center in Fort Walton Beach had a linoleum tile floor with fan shaped metal backboards. The court where we were going to play had a new hardwood floor with glass backboards. The basketball bounces very differently on wood and getting use to glass backboards when you have been shooting at metal backboards could take a week or so. The team looked great in their new uniforms and played their hearts out. We lost to the eventual champions in our first game. The season had been great and the boys learned a lot more than just how to play good basketball.

If It's Spring, It Must Be Baseball

It was in the spring of 1965 when a phone message was left for me to call a major on the main base at Eglin. I worked at Field 3, about fifteen miles from the main base. He was in charge of the youth baseball league at Eglin. He said that he had heard about my basketball team and wondered if I had ever coached baseball. When I told him that I had played baseball and softball for years and coached while in college, he asked if I would coach a team in the "Little Minor League." He explained that after tryouts, the boys were divided into two groups based upon skill level. The better players were to play in the "Little Major League" and the less capable players were to populate the "Little Minor League." I have always been up to a challenge and answered that I would coach a team. Only then did he further explain that teams were picked by the coaches after several workouts. There was a draft system in which the coaches chose players in rotation until the team rosters had been filled. The bomb then dropped! No one had chosen 23 of the players who were to play in the little minor league. You guessed it—the 23 boys were my team.

I was the only coach. I had no assistant coaches. I was depressed. The players could be as young as 8 and as old as 12. I had one 12 year old, one 11 year old, two 10 year olds and the rest were either 8 or 9. The only ray of sunshine was an interesting rule about brothers. If you drafted a player with a brother or brothers, you got all of them. The only 12 year old was undrafted because he had 8 and 9 year old brothers. I was even more disheartened to discover that the 8 year old was really only 6 years and 10 months old.

Organizing a practice for 23 players is akin to herding cats. My first job was to assess what skill levels existed, if any. I had two players who professed to be catchers, Johnny and Clay. Andy, the 12 year old, was the only player who said he was a pitcher. I put everyone except Clay and Johnny in right field. Each player had to make a throw to home plate and one to second base. When that was done, we started over and repeated the process. I needed for three pitchers and a shortstop. I then divided them into two groups, one at shortstop and one at first base. I was looking for players who could throw people out from the infield and people who could catch the ball when it was thrown to them. The next test was a series of races to see who could run. You can hide slow guys at first base and catcher if you have to do so, but only if they can hit. That was all I could handle the first day. My group of players made the "Bad News Bears" look like champions. Determining if anyone could hit the ball would be relegated to the second practice.

I pondered how in the world I could even have batting practice with 23 kids. Then I had an idea that I thought just might work. I bought a dozen baseballs and went to the local Ace Hardware store. I bought a dozen 3½ inch eye bolts with metal rings on one end, a dozen nuts and lock washers and 90 feet of water ski tow rope. From there I was off to the base machine shop where I drilled holes through each baseball, carefully avoiding the seams. I loaded up all of my stuff and headed home to assemble my batting practice devices. An eye bolt was inserted through each of the baseballs. A lock washer and a nut secured the bolt to each baseball. A 15 foot length of ski rope was attached through the eye of each bolt.

My idea was to have four players in a circle at the 12, 3, 6 and 9 o'clock positions. One player would stand in the middle of the circle and swing the baseball around on the end of the rope so that the ball would be in a position for the players to hit it. The players would take turns trying to hit the ball as it swung around. There would be four circles going simultaneously. Sixteen batters, four swingers and three evaluators would round out the number of players on the team. I would be the fourth evaluator. I demonstrated how it would work at the next practice. After having watched them throw and run I guessed who would be the best hitters. Andy, Johnny, Clay and Phillip filled out the demonstration team. Andy and Phillip proved to be the best hitters followed by Johnny and Clay.

The practice device had advantages I had not even thought about. I could make the pitch approach the hitter high, low, inside, outside or down the middle. The ball was never coming on a straight line as it would when thrown from the mound. It was more like a slow curve ball in how it approached the batter. Much more concentration was required to hit the ball than if it had been thrown normally. We set up the circles and started batting practice. I was disappointed at what poor hitters I had on the team. Without an alternate strategy, my team would lead the league in strikeouts. I created three categories of batters: Lookers, Bunters and Swingers. Lookers would not be allowed to swing or bunt until they had graduated to the Bunters group. Bunters could not swing at the ball until they had graduated to the Swingers group. Swingers were allowed to swing unless I had on the "take sign" or the "bunt sign." Being a Looker was somewhat like being an "Untouchable" in India. We only had one Looker who never graduated to being a Bunter. His status as a Looker was something very special. It was six year old Roy who walked on every at bat until the last game when I let him swing after we had wrapped up the game. When Roy went into the crouch position I had taught him, it was like trying to throw strikes to a mole. We won several games when I pinch hit Roy to get a walk which resulted in a run being scored.

It was a week before our first game and I only had four swingers. Three bunters and two lookers rounded out the starting lineup. Of the nine teams in our league, we had the smallest number of talented players. I would be starting the youngest team in the history of the league. I received a call from a major whose son was on the team. His son was barely 8 and was the second smallest player on the team. He expressed concern that his son might get turned off on sports because he would not get to play. He was thinking of taking his son off of the team so he wouldn't be disappointed. I told the major he might want to come to a practice and attend the first game. I shared with him that his son was the starting second baseman and the second-ranked pitcher on the team. "Meatball," as his teammates called him had a really strong arm for an 8 year old. His point of delivery was about at the batters knees. I didn't see him throw a single pitch all season which was more than a couple of inches higher than the batter's knees. Years later I saw him often at SMU basketball games where he was the team's manager.

The game plan for the first game was simple. Roy, our diminutive looker, would draw a walk. I would put in a pinch runner. Our best bunter would try to move the runner to second base. The two best swingers batted third and fourth. That strategy produced two runs in the first inning. Another looker followed the swingers, followed by our second best bunter. The third and fourth best hitters followed the second bunter. One more run scored and we led the game 3 to 0 after our first at bat. I discovered that our bunters had just as good a chance of getting on base as our swingers. Later in the year we would bunt seven consecutive times and get on base six of those times.

We were ahead 3 to 0, when our secret weapon went to the mound. Andy, our one 12 year old, was the only pitcher in the little minor league who could throw a curve ball. It scared the dickens out of the other team's players. Nine pitches, three outs and we were ready to come to the plate again.

As the season wore on, we became more adept at hitting, bunting, running the bases and playing defense. We had the smoothest fielding shortstop in the league in Phillip. Phillip was on the team because his step-brother, Larry, was mildly retarded. No one wanted Phillip bad enough to take Larry. Bobby had taught me that every player could contribute to the team and it was my job to figure out how Larry could do it. He was the largest player on the team and was also the strongest. The backstop of the field where we played was chicken wire, not the chain link fence that you usually see on little league fields. I discovered by accident that Larry could throw the ball through the chicken wire. I decided to allow Larry to warm up as though he was going to pitch before the game started. He was as wild as a March hare. After a few warm up pitches, one of which would be missed on purpose so it could go through the backstop, our catcher, either Johnny or Clay, would come up to me and loudly say, "Coach, you can't let Larry pitch, he might kill somebody." I would go out to the mound and take the ball from Larry and call either Andy or Meatball to the mound. The first few hitters on the other team would still be in shock when the game started.

When Larry played, it was always in right field. If the ball went into right field, the first baseman would run into the outfield and tell Larry where to throw the ball. On one occasion, there was a runner on second base who tried to score on a single to right field. The first baseman ran into the field and told Larry to throw the ball to the catcher. As the runner rounded third base and headed home, Larry unleashed a mighty throw toward home plate. As the runner slid into home plate, the throw cleared the backstop, the stands and crashed through the windshield of a car three rows back in the parking lot!

Looking back on all of my years of working with youth sports teams, I think I did the best job of coaching with that team of 23 rag-tag players. Before the season was over, we were playing great baseball. We finished second in the league of nine teams. As I was told years later by the famous Red Auerbach, coach of the NBA Boston Celtics, "Luck is what you find at the intersection of hard work and opportunity." No one thought that we had a chance, except us.

Back to Basketball

The next experience I want to share with you occurred after I graduated from law school. We had moved to far north Dallas, in the Richardson Independent School District. The youth sports organization in that area was the Spring Valley Athletic Association, SVAA. I agreed to coach an eighth grade basketball team. Many of the teams kept their same players as they passed on to the next grade. The players would be kids who enjoyed playing basketball, but were not good enough to play for their school team. The teams had been selected by the SVAA prior to my agreeing to coach. I met my players at the gym for our first practice on a Saturday morning in October. There were only five players. I explained that we needed at least eight players on the team. One of my best players was an orthodox Jewish boy who could not play on Saturdays. At least half of our games were scheduled for Saturday. I asked each of the team members to bring another player to the next practice. I told them I wanted them to bring the fastest, the strongest, the tallest, and the meanest kid in their class who was not on the school team or on another team in our league. They responded almost in unison that there was only one kid who fit that description. I asked why he was not playing on the school team. They explained that he had beaten up the school coach. I asked them to bring him and at least three others to the next practice.

At the next practice, there were three new players who wanted to be a part of our team. I had not seen anyone who matched the description of the player I really wanted to see. Then an outside door opened and a young black man came into the gym. His full Afro brushed against the door closing arm. He walked straight up to me and said," I hear you're looking for me." Clint was 14 years old, 6'4" tall and weighed at least 225 pounds. He looked like he had been chiseled out of marble. I looked him straight in the eye and asked, "Do you want to learn how to play ball?" "Yeah," he replied. This would be the first time I had ever coached a player of color. And I had never seen a player with the raw talent of Clint. I had played center at 6'2" during my junior year in high school. I could show Clint some basic moves around the basket. He was not a quick learner and had to have numerous repetitions in order to learn how to use his brute strength around the basket.

The offense was designed to take advantage of Clint's size and strength. He had soft hands and was able to handle passes from different angles. Part of my challenge was to teach the other players how to get the ball to Clint in positions close to the basket. Several of my guards had the tendency to shoot rather than to work the ball into Clint down low near the goal. Our practices went well and we were excited about our first game.

The game started with Clint getting the tip to one of our guards. Clint set up low in the lane and signaled for the ball. Instead of passing the ball to Clint, the guard jacked up a twenty foot shot which rebounded to our opponents. Clint scowled as he ran down the court to play defense. Clint blocked our opponents first shot and our forward retrieved the ball and passed off to the guard coming down the court. Our forward set a screen for Clint, who was in position to receive a pass and easily score. Instead, our guard put up a twenty foot shot which clanged off of the backboard into the hands of an opposing player. Fortunately, our opponents missed their second shot which Clint rebounded and called time out.

I was irritated at the guards who had not even tried to get the ball to Clint. We huddled up and I told Clint, "The next time we come down the court and a guard shoots without trying to get the ball into you, I want you to hit him between the shoulder blades on the way back down the court to the other team's basket." The guard who was guilty of the last shot protested, "Coach, he will hurt one of us really bad if he hits us." "He will only have to hurt one of you. The others will learn to pass him the ball," I said. I couldn't believe that the next time down the court, the other guard shot the ball without even looking inside to Clint. The first "Thud" occurred when Clint hit his teammate. The second "Thud" occurred when the guard hit the floor. The referee immediately blew his whistle and called a foul on Clint. I quickly explained that no foul could occur unless Clint hit an opposing player. The two referees huddled and reversed the foul and gave the ball to our opponents.

The rest of the game went as planned. Every time down the court, our players worked the ball into Clint. He scored 26 points and got 18 rebounds. We went through the schedule undefeated.

Clint's Mother was very tall. His grandfather was seven feet tall. Clint grew to 6'9" and played football in high school and college. He later played offensive tackle in the National Football League for a number of years. He was a kid in a man's body when I coached him. I learned a lot from working with Clint. I was able to use that knowledge in helping other kids develop both physical and emotional skills needed to compete in sports and in life.

My greatest sports adventure came about for a very unusual reason. The Dallas Thomas Jefferson High School basketball team participated in several state championship tournaments in Texas in the sixties. One year, their coach, Archie Porter, took his team to a camp in Buena Vista, Colorado to practice for a month during the summer. Thomas Jefferson dominated the highest division in Texas high schools the next season and won the state championship. After another visit to the Colorado camp, the team repeated its domination in Texas the following year. In what many believed to be an overreaction, the University of Texas Interscholastic League passed a rule stating that if you attended a basketball summer camp, you would be ineligible to play for your high school.

Ignorant of the rule, Dave Cowens, all-pro center of the Boston Celtics, and Rudy Tomjonavich, all–pro forward of the Houston Rockets, purchased a basketball camp in Texas. I received a call from SMU coach, Sonny Allen, inquiring about whether I would be interested in challenging the UIL rule. I responded that I was very interested, but that in order to be successful, we would need "the right kid." The UIL rule put Texas high school players at a serious disadvantage when competing with players from other states. The disadvantage was not only a severe restriction that prohibited them from playing against elite players from other states, but it also seriously impacted their chance to receive basketball scholarships to college. The ideal kid would have to be a high school junior who stood to lose his senior season of competition if he attended a basketball summer camp.

The word was out that we needed the right kid if the challenge to the rule stood a chance. Several months after talking to coach Allen, a third-year law student from Arizona called me. He informed me that he knew the perfect kid for the case. The young man was 6'11" tall and weighed 250 pounds. He was president of the student body of his school as a junior and had just made a 1480 on his college entrance exams. I called Coach Allen, who called Dave Cowens, who called me. Dave and I agreed to meet in Houston to interview the young man.

We met Greg Kite and his family at seven o'clock in the restaurant of the hotel where we were staying. Dave had asked for Greg to bring some film of him playing for his high school. Greg was two inches taller than Dave and probably thirty pounds heavier. Greg was intelligent and extremely well spoken. I could see that he would make an excellent witness. Although he had been all-pro for a number of years, Dave Cowens was one of the most down to earth people I had ever met. He was totally unimpressed with himself. He would prove to be one of the most effective witnesses I have seen on the stand in my forty-five years of law practice. After dinner, we adjourned to a room for Dave to watch the film of Greg playing. After watching for a few minutes, Dave asked Greg, "Do you have a basketball in your car?" After Greg replied in the affirmative, Dave asked, "Do you know where there is a lighted court?" At about 10:00 p.m. we set off for a lighted basketball court. The lesson lasted about thirty minutes. Back at the hotel, Dave and I agreed that Greg would be the perfect "kid" for the challenge to the UIL rule.

The suit was filed in Federal court in Houston. I

158

requested a Temporary Restraining Order against the University Interscholastic League in order for Greg to go to a basketball summer camp without retribution from the UIL. The UIL was represented by Attorney General John Hill who was later to be the Chief Justice of the Texas Supreme Court. I had met Attorney General Hill years before when he was brought in to try the airplane crash case I described in the chapter on my second year in law school.

The hearing on the Temporary Restraining Order was entertaining. I called Dave Cowens as my first witness. The questioning went as follows:

Q: Would you state your name for the record?

A: David Cowens

Q: What is your profession or occupation?

A: I am a worker for the Boston Celtics.

Seeing how things were going and not liking to lose, Attorney General Hill did not show up for the final hearing and arguments. We were successful in getting an injunction against the UIL. It was a great victory for me personally, for Greg Kite, for Dave Cowens and for Texas high school basketball.

Greg went to summer camp and led his team to the state semi-finals in his senior year. He attended Brigham Young University where he became an All-American player. Next, he was the number one draft choice of the Boston Celtics. He was a member of the Celtics for six years before he was traded to the Orlando Magic, where he was the backup center to Shaquille O'Neal for the balance of his career.

After Greg signed with the Celtics, I became their unofficial restaurant guide when they played the Dallas Mavericks. Taking the Celtics to the Southern Kitchen and Sonny Bryan's Smokehouse are two of my favorite memories. As a life-long basketball junkie, it was a thrill to meet Bob Cousy, Bill Russell, Arnold, "Red," Auerbach, K.C. Jones, Larry Bird, Kevin McHale, Jo Jo White, Cornbread Maxwell, Robert Parrish, Denny Ainge, Hank Wedman, Fred Roberts and other team members.

The right for parents to direct their children's education during the time school is not in session is now a firmly established principle in Texas. Our victory was even sweeter because the UIL and the Texas attorney general had acted with unbelievable arrogance and had treated me with total disrespect during the entire proceeding. Texas was the only state in the nation that had a prohibition against high school basketball players attending summer camps.

Other states, such as Illinois, had rules that prohibited players from going to a camp where their coach worked. The Texas UIL steadfastly refused to consider a change in their rules to allow players to improve their individual skills, even if there were safeguards which would prevent a team from having all or many of its players attend the same camp.

I was flattered recently when a very famous college and professional basketball coach told me that in his opinion I had made the single greatest contribution to the development of Texas high school basketball in history. He told me that because of the ruling which had allowed players to go to camp and play during the summer on AAU teams, Texas was producing tremendous talent which had been previously stifled by the unreasonable rules of the University Interscholastic League.

MORE CASES

Where Have All the Exhibits Gone?

The call came from my future client's father. His daughter wanted a divorce. She was being treated in a mental health facility. She had lost over thirty pounds in the few months before starting inpatient treatment. She was married to a Texas district court judge and had two sons. She had been little help to her therapists in determining the cause of her problems. One therapist suggested that hypnosis might help her release her thoughts and feelings. To her therapist's great amazement, he learned of a course of conduct that caused his patient to repress her feelings and memories.

Her husband had a significant problem with pornography. He would bring home XXXX-rated video tapes and make her act out what was on the videos. He had purchased whips, restraints, dildos, vibrators and books of colored pictures depicting every imaginable sexual act. There were homosexual depictions of males, females and combinations. Once the wife was able to describe what had been happening, we had to be able to prove it in court.

Periodically, she was released from her treatment center to see her sons and her family. Therefore, she was able to get into the house while her husband was hearing cases as a judge. I have never thought of myself as either naïve or uninformed, but I had never seen or even heard about some of the things she removed from her husband's closet.

There was a logistical problem. We did not want the case to be heard in the district where the judge presided. At the same time, we realized that there would probably be a natural prejudice in favor of the judge by most other sitting judges. The petition for divorce was filed with language that was as innocuous as possible. There was no need to plead facts which would embarrass the judge. Our client's father was a prominent business man who wanted the best team possible for his daughter. I associated Donald R. Smith to work with me. I believed Don to be the best family law trial attorney in Texas. He was a combination of legal scholar, revival preacher and machine gun. Don could say more, faster than anyone I have ever seen in court.

When the judge was served with the divorce petition, he hired two of the best family law attorneys from his part of the state. All of the attorneys had known each other for a number of years. We agreed to have the case tried in a district which was significantly removed from the one where the judge held court. And we agreed on the trial judge whom we believed to be one of the best family law judges in Texas. The challenge was to convince the judge to hear the case. It would be a contested custody case with complex property issues.

The judge asked us, "Why in the world would I want to try this case?" One of our opposing counsel explained, "It is because you are the only judge all of us trust to do a good job." He agreed to hear the case and appointed one of the most respected family lawyers in the state to represent the children. After a significant period of discovery and evaluation by experts, the case was set for trial.

Our client's father sent his private plane to Dallas to pick up his daughter's attorneys and fly us to the city where the trial would take place. We arrived the day before the trial was to begin and spent the better part of the day going over the order of witnesses and prepping our client to testify. All of our trial exhibits were loaded into the trunk of our rental car the night before the trial.

Then our client, her dad and her two attorneys went to dinner together. We had a very pleasant meal at a fine restaurant. After dinner, we all went back to our car to return to our hotel. As we approached the car, I was immediately apprehensive. The trunk of our rental car had been "popped." As a kid who grew up in a federal housing project, I had seen people "pop" the trunk of a car with a hammer and a screw driver. The screw driver was placed in key slot and hit with the hammer. The lock would be punched into the trunk and the trunk would pop open. ALL OF OUR TRIAL EXHIBITS HAD BEEN TAKEN! My co-counsel was ashen white. "What are we going to do?" he asked.

I turned to our client's father and said, "I need a thousand dollars cash." "Why?" he responded. I explained, "I am going to take your daughter to a porno shop and we are going to buy one of everything they have stolen. They may have had the guts to steal our exhibits, but they won't have the guts to object to our exhibits by saying "those can't be the real exhibits because we stole them."

My co-counsel would not go exhibit-shopping with me. Our client was a bit leery of my plan. She and I got in the rental car and headed off to the street where most of the porno shops were located. She helped me identify the sex toys that had been stolen. We even picked out a few new items which she thought might really get under her husband's skin. We selected whips, handcuffs, dildos, vibrators and color magazines with graphic depiction of wide variety of sexual acts.

When we were checking out, the young man at the register, whose sexual preference was not in question, stated, "You have been such great customers—would you like some free batteries for the vibrators?" It was the first time I had ever seen my client smile. I said, "Thanks, but we are not going to use them for the reason you might imagine." We stopped at a Safeway store on the way back to the hotel and got a couple of grocery sacks into which we put our new exhibits. When I got back to my room, I marked them with exhibit stickers. Then I dropped off to sleep wondering if my grand plan would succeed.

After a light breakfast, we were off to court. The look on one opposing attorney's face was something to behold when he saw me carrying my two Safeway sacks of exhibits into the courtroom. It was obvious to me that he did not expect to see any exhibits like the ones in my grocery sacks. I had created an exhibit log which we had exchanged with opposing counsel. The "new exhibits" were marked in that exact order of the log.

After a few formalities, we called our client as our first witness. I took her through some background questions about her husband's conduct. After having received permission to approach the witness, I handed her a large dildo, which was marked as exhibit one. She identified it for the court. When I offered it to the court for admission in evidence, there was no objection by opposing counsel. So far, so good I thought as I handed my client a pair of handcuffs—identified, offered and admitted without objection. My next exhibit was a small whip that looked almost like a crop one might use on a horse—identified, offered and admitted without objection.

The judge rose from his chair and said, "I want to see counsel in chambers." All of us followed the judge out the back door of the courtroom and into his chambers. He looked directly at me and said, "Charles, you have already convinced me that he is the kinkiest SOB I have ever had in my court. Keep the rest of that crap in those sacks and take them off of the counsel table!"

The rest of the morning was taken up in direct and cross-examination of our client. At one point my co-counsel was responding to an objection made by opposing counsel. The judge looked at my co-counsel and asked, "Do you think I am going deaf? Well I'm not and you need to tone down your voice." We all admired the judge, partially because he was very plain spoken, but also because he kept control of his courtroom without trying to embarrass either the attorneys or the parties. We recessed for lunch after a three hour morning session.

The attorney for the sons suggested that all the attorneys talk before going to lunch. He remarked to the four of us, "This case needs to be settled now." With his help, the matter was resolved during the lunch break. What had been scheduled as a five-day trial was over before the afternoon session. The judge was very pleased. Neither of the parties was completely happy. If either party to a case is totally happy, it means that someone's ox just got gored. You must always be willing to compromise if it means accepting a result which is between the "best case" and "worst case" parameters.

Back in my office, I faced an interesting dilemma. What in the world was I going to do with the exhibits? Should I just throw them in the trash? I called a staff meeting, which included the receptionist, secretaries, legal assistants and attorneys. I told them that I was going to put all of the exhibits on the library table and then go to lunch. I explained that I did not care who took what. I just wanted the library table to be cleared off when I returned from lunch. When I came back from lunch, my request had been granted.

The Shrine

I have few prejudices against groups of people. Growing up in a neighborhood of mostly poor folks convinced me that all people who have few resources have the same kinds of problems. Race means very little to me. I have enjoyed helping people irrespective of their color, race or religion. However, I have developed a very deep prejudice against anyone who does not treat women with respect. The women in my family all have been intelligent, educated and successful. One of my aunts was the first woman to become a high school principal in Texas. My wife and her sister, Sydney, are great examples of how women contribute to our society through their influence on their respective professions.

I have experienced what I believe to be a pattern of denigration of women by men from Eastern Europe, the Middle East, India and Pakistan. I have enthusiastically participated in women's rights cases during my legal career. Several of my attempts to support women's rights have been in cases which have gone to the Texas Supreme Court. I am proud that the law of Texas has been changed by the cases which I have handled supporting women's rights.

The lady who came into my office was already weeping before she took a seat opposite my desk. She had been born in India. Her parents had arranged her marriage to a prominent scientist working for a large Dallas company. He had a Ph.D. from an excellent university and was highly paid by his corporation. She told me that they had been married for several years. She had received her first degree from a university in India. Her master's degree was earned in England. She was enrolled in a doctoral program at the University of Texas in Dallas. Despite her education, her husband wanted her to stay at home, cook his meals and clean his house. She shared with me that he was verbally and physically abusive. I asked her for an example of his physical abuse. Between sobs, she told me of a recent incident when he had been going northbound on Central Expressway in Dallas. He was angry with her about her requests to work outside of the home. He exited the freeway and proceeded to the first signal light on the frontage road. He stopped the car at the light, reached down and released her seat belt, then reached across her and opened the passenger door and kicked her out of the car onto the street. He drove off, leaving her lying in the road beside the curb.

After we discussed her options, she decided to file for divorce. The petition was fairly innocuous. She insisted that she did not want any property; she only wanted to be free from her abusive husband. It reminded me of the old quote from the mouse, "I really don't want the cheese; I just want to get out of the trap." She had no independent means of support and had never been allowed access to any bank accounts or credit cards during her marriage. Fortunately, her parents were both medical doctors in India as were her brothers. There were funds available to help her get by during the divorce proceeding. I ask for basic discovery and disclosure of information about the couple's assets. To my great surprise, retirement benefits and stock options of substantial value had been acquired during their marriage. Investment accounts and money market accounts also existed.

I was contacted by my client's father who lived in Delhi, India. He was very concerned about his daughter's well-being. He wanted me to do everything possible to see that she was treated fairly. I scheduled a settlement conference with the husband's attorney. Even though the husband denied that he had been physically abusive, pictures taken at the hospital the night my client was kicked out of their car helped enlighten his counsel. Messages from the husband to my client clearly showed that he considered her his property to do with as he saw fit.

In Texas either side of a divorce case can request a jury trial. I told opposing counsel of our intention to make that request. The function of the jury is to determine facts. The judge decides questions of law and how the facts should be interpreted based upon the law. I thought the husband would have a tough time selling his story to a jury which had at least six women. Apparently he did too. The case never got to trial. It was settled on very favorable terms to my client.

A week or so later, I got a phone call from Delhi, India. My client's father was effusive in his praise of my efforts on behalf of his daughter. He shared with me that my client's settlement exceeded the amount of money he and his wife had accumulated during their working lives as doctors. He told me that he had a small shrine built in a room of their house in my honor. He explained that they planned to burn incense once a month to honor me and to celebrate what I had done for their daughter. He invited me to come to Delhi for a visit. Unfortunately, I've never been able to accept his invitation but I have stayed in contact with them.

The last time I heard from my client was when she called to tell me that she had received her doctorate degree and was teaching at her college. She also told me that she had been seeing a very nice man who treated her well.

The Ultimate Gigolo

He was an educated, sophisticated gentleman with a tremendous fund of knowledge about art, music, literature and world events. He was fluent in at least four languages. He was a renowned scholar who had over a dozen published books on topics of religion and philosophy. He was considered to be an expert on the Old Testament. His father had been the president of a prestigious university on the east coast of the United States. He had undergraduate and graduate degrees in English and Creative Writing from well-respected universities. His appearance was also impressive. His full head of hair had turned to a silver-white color.

Harry Lee had spent all of his adult life as a companion to very wealthy women whose families were members of the elite social circles in the towns where they lived. He was a GIGOLO. His first patron had found him when he was still in his early twenties. He was a delightful companion, dancing partner and lover. His patron was considerably older than Harry. Having an age difference with his lady friends would become the rule, rather than the exception.

I became acquainted with Harry Lee for a most interesting reason. He had been living in luxury for all of his adult life. After the death of his second patron, he became close to the lady with whom he would live for most of his later life. He was in his sixties when he called me for advice. He had been living in a high-rise apartment at one of the most prestigious addresses on Turtle Creek for about thirty years when his companion died. At the time of her death, she was in her late eighties. She had a large apartment on one of the upper floors of the high-rise. For appearance's sake, she had purchased a smaller unit on the floor directly below her residence and put a circular staircase up to her apartment in a closet. Harry Lee supposedly lived in the lower unit. His patron was extremely wealthy. In her later years, she had a full time nurse to take care of her medical and personal needs. She had made provision in her will for Harry Lee to benefit substantially upon her death. Her devoted nurse was also treated generously in her will.

She and Harry Lee had enjoyed traveling to many parts of the world together. Before intercontinental airline flight was common, they had crossed the Atlantic Ocean so many times on the S.S. France that the steamship line presented them with an eight foot model of the ship. Harry Lee was as devoted to her as she was to him.

When she died, her family challenged the bequest to Harry Lee. The amount she had intended for him was well into seven figures. Many of the property principles of family law apply whether in a divorce or a probate proceeding. Harry Lee came to consult with me about his rights under the will. I explained the concept of informal marriage to him and suggested that I contact the attorney for the family about resolving the dispute. When I explained to the family's probate attorney that I thought there was an excellent chance that two adults who had lived together for almost thirty years might be informally married under Texas law, he was taken aback. I suggested that if the family didn't challenge the bequest to Harry Lee, he would not raise the question of informal marriage. Had the court found that an informal marriage existed, the exposure would have been a minimum of ten times the bequest. After a period of time, both Harry Lee and the nurse received the amounts left to them in their benefactor's will.

A miraculous thing happened. Harry Lee and the nurse had become close friends during the few years before the lady's death. Neither had ever been ceremonially married. Harry Lee called to tell me that they were going to get married and move to the San Francisco area. The next thing I heard was that they had purchased a home in the Sausalito hills overlooking the Golden Gate Bridge and San Francisco Bay.

Several years later my wife and I were planning a trip to San Francisco to visit with the editor of my book, "Texas Family Law Trial Guide." I called and mentioned to Harry Lee that I would be in San Francisco and would love to see him. He invited us to come to his house for a visit while in the area. Although I never used the names of clients, I had told Ann about this remarkable man who had a way with women which astonished me. He was charming, caring, and funny and had the ability to make women feel really good about themselves. He would complement them on their perfume by its name and on their dresses by the name of the line or designer. I never figured out how he knew so much about everything. I was looking forward to seeing him and Ann wanted to find out whether I had been exaggerating about Harry Lee over the years.

After a morning meeting with my editor, we took a driving tour of San Francisco. From the wharf to the Golden Gate Bridge to Russian Hill to cable car rides to the Ghirardelli chocolate factory and everything in between, we soaked in the sights of San Francisco. The day was cool and windy with a little fog thrown in for good measure. Time had gotten away from us. I suggested that it was time to start driving to Sausalito to see Harry Lee. Ann protested that she needed to go back to the hotel to freshen up and do something with her hair. But I insisted that we head across the Golden Gate Bridge to Harry Lee's house. We had a little trouble locating his house, but finally pulled into his driveway. He came out to the car and went to Ann's door. He opened the door, took her hand, kissed it and said, "I knew you would be pretty, I didn't know you would be beautiful." Harry Lee's charm strikes again.

Ann later conceded that everything I had told her about Harry Lee's ability to impress the ladies was probably understated. His house was very attractive, but the view of the Golden Gate Bridge, San Francisco Bay and Alcatraz Island was breath taking. There was a model of the S.S. France on a sofa table.. We had a glass of wine, and some cheese and crackers while we visited. Harry Lee insisted that he show us his new cape that had been made for him to wear to the opera. It was made of black silk, lined with bright red velvet. I am sure that he looked quite dashing while wearing the cape over his black tuxedo. His wife was charming. They seemed very happy together. He was not the only gigolo I have encountered in my years of law practice, but he was certainly the classiest.

Send for the Photographer

I got a call from a long-time civil attorney friend asking me if I could help on a complex divorce case. I have always been interested in complex rather than simple. I set up an appointment to meet my new client. Like Harry Lee, he was a handsome sixty-plus year-old with a head full of silver-white hair. I was envious immediately because I was already losing my hair in my late forties. He was an interesting fellow with an amazing life history. He had been orphaned as a young boy. He earned a meager living by collecting fruit jars in the oil fields of east Texas and returning them to bootleggers for a penny per jar. He was a tough kid who survived on his own for years. At fourteen, he lied about his age, joined the Marine Corps and fought in World War II. He eventually became a pilot and downed several enemy planes over Germany. He had never attended school, but was able to get into college and get a degree in geology. After graduation, he went back to the oil fields and started to make a small fortune. He married and moved from east Texas to Dallas where he lived in the affluent Park Cities. He had expanded his business interests to include many other activities in addition to his oil business. Shortly before our meeting, he had a planned business trip to North Africa which did not occur as expected.

He had left his Park Cities home to go to the airport. His trip included talking to some of the most powerful individuals in Africa about oil and gas deals which could potentially make him another fortune. After waiting at the airport for several hours, his flight was cancelled. Frustrated because he would not be able to keep appointments that had taken months to schedule, he took a cab back to his house. When he arrived, he saw a car he did not recognize in front of the house. He told me that he was immediately suspicious about the situation. He had the cab go around the corner and take him to the area near the rear of his house. He was a black belt in karate and had a home gym that rivaled the best in town. He scaled the back wall and crawled on his belly toward the back of the house where the master bedroom was located. When he got to the house, he could see his wife in bed with one of the most prominent members of the Dallas arts community. Being a man of action, he grabbed a wrought iron chair and threw it through the sliding glass doors of the bedroom. He entered the bedroom quickly and retrieved a pistol from a nearby chest of drawers.

He leveled the pistol at his wife's lover and told him to sit on the bench at the end of the bed. He made his wife join her lover on the bench. He then made a phone call to a professional photographer and instructed him to come to the house immediately. At one point in time the lover decided to make a run for it, although nude. A quick shot rang over his head and buried itself in the bedroom wall. He obediently sat back down on the bench.

The photographer arrived soon after the attempted escape. Almost twenty pictures were taken in short order. My favorites were the two in which the lover had a bra over his head with the cups covering his ears and when he was modeling one of the wife's nightgowns. When the photo shoot was over, the two were made to walk out the front door of the house in the nude and go to the lover's car.

My new client brought the pictures to our consultation. He asked me, "Do you think the pictures will help." I told him that the way in which he acquired the pictures might hurt a little, but they would help us settle the case. He was a smooth talking rascal and acted twenty years younger than his chronological age. His case settled without having to go to court a single time.

The day of his divorce, a well-known Hollywood actress flew into town to spend the weekend with my client. He was fond of her, but he didn't want to be known as Mr. Hollywood star. He wouldn't have fit in that well in Los Angeles.

He decided there were too many bad memories at his old place so he hired a realtor to help him find a new place. He called me and said that he wanted me to be at the closing of the new purchase at 5:00 a.m. I ask him why in the world he needed to close the deal that early. He explained that the house he was buying was painted pink and that no one would ever be able to say that he lived in a pink house. He had three crews of painters ready to start painting at 6:00 a.m. Before the sun set, the house was a very attractive light gray.

This gentleman makes the "Most Interesting Man in the World," who drinks Dos Equis in the beer commercial, look like a sissy. Several years before I helped him, he had threatened to kill Muammar Gaddafi when he thought he was being cheated in an oil deal in Libya. I have often thought he could have saved the U.S. a lot of time and money.

I heard from him about eight years later. He called to offer his help to a lady I was representing. He said he had been dating her twenty-eight year old daughter. By this time he had to be seventy. He said his young girlfriend had told him that that her step-father was being cruel to her mother. He asked me," Would it help if I had some of my boys tie him (the husband) to a tree and beat him with a chain?" I thanked him for his interest, but declined his offer.

"Give Me That Rock and Roll Music"

Once in a great while I get the opportunity to try and fix a mess that someone else has made. This one was a real doozy. The case stands out for several reasons. My client was in the music business. He had started out as a roadie who helped set up the stage and the sound system for concerts. He was not educated, but he was clever when it came to the music business. Over a period of years he had become a rock concert promoter who worked with many of the top bands in the country. His company and its success had been noticed by two of the "big boys" in Los Angeles. I will refer to them as Frank and Danny. They offered to include my client in a partnership which would own the largest company in the United States that promoted concerts and tours of leading singing groups and bands.

As I learned, the promoter of an event typically provided young ladies and refreshments for the performers. If the promoter did not do a good job in this part of the business, he often lost the musical group to another promoter. My client met one of the young ladies who had been hired to provide companionship to the band. He was smitten with her. Her beautiful eyes and shiny hair were not her principal attractions. He invited her to Dallas to share his accommodations. They very much enjoyed each other's company and lived together in unwedded bliss.

A high-rolling entertainment attorney in California was preparing the partnership documents. He heard about the blithe spirit back in Texas and knew that Texas recognized common law marriage. He didn't want to take a chance that the young lady would clutter up the business deal by alleging that she was a common law wife with an interest in the partnership. He advised my client to marry his companion and then file for divorce the next day. He lined up an entertainment attorney in Texas to file the divorce.

The plan concocted by the California attorney would have worked out in the "land of fruits and nuts," but it was fatally flawed in Texas. In California, once a divorce petition is filed, property acquired after that date is not community property subject to division at the time of divorce. In Texas, community property continues to accumulate until the divorce is granted. After the word that the Texas divorce had been filed, the partnership documents were executed making my client partners with Frank and Danny.

A day or so after the partnership documents had been executed, I got a call from the Dallas entertainment attorney asking if I would take over and finalize the divorce, which he described as a "no brainer." I agreed to take over the case, but I did not realize until I learned the facts the extent to which it was a "no brainer." Not knowing the law of another state and assuming that it is the same as your state's law is guaranteed to get you in trouble. To add insult to injury, the castaway bride hired a very skilled family law attorney who smelled blood in the water. And blood in the water there was.

The attorney for the wife filed a counter-petition. My client needed to be served with a citation notifying him that his wife had filed the counter-petition. He was traveling a great deal of the time with his concerts. He also might have been avoiding service of process.

During my legal career I had seen some examples of service of process which I thought were in poor taste. In one case the husband had been served with a citation at his mother's funeral. In another case, the wife had rented a billboard on Central Expressway, announcing she was divorcing her "worthless husband." Another husband had hired an airplane to pull a banner behind plane announcing the divorce. The creativity of service in this case reached an all-time high. My client was in town for a concert. He had gone back to his hotel room afterward. It was late when there was a knock at his door. He went to the door to find a beautiful young lady in a very revealing dress. She explained that she was one of the girls he had hired to comfort the band members after their concert. She went on to tell him that the drummer had already connected with another lady. She asked him, "Do you want me to come in and comfort you?" Being a red-blooded American boy, he invited her into his room. After having what he described as unbelievable sex, she reached behind her under the pillow, pulled out a citation, handed it to him, smiled and said, "Now you have been screwed twice." She dressed quickly and left.

He had been served and ordered to appear in court the next Tuesday. The case was really complicated by the advice of the California attorney to marry his live-in friend. It ended up costing him a bunch of money. His wife's attorney was driving a new Mercedes after the case concluded. There were a series of settlement meetings which alternated from my office to opposing counsel's office. At the last settlement conference, which occurred at wife's counsel's office, we were only fifty thousand dollars apart. My client asked if the two parties could talk alone to try to reach a compromise. I said I didn't have a problem with that and her attorney agreed. They went to a conference room down the hall.

About thirty minutes later they returned and announced that he would pay the money she wanted. I asked him later why he agreed. He smiled broadly and said, "I told her if we could have sex just one last time, she could have the damn money. She was the best I ever had."

About six months later, I received a message from my client's ex-wife to check out the ad on page 23 of the current issue of Playboy magazine. She was lying on a red satin sheet with nothing on except very expensive diamond jewelry. The ad was tasteful in that she was lying on her tummy and all that was exposed was her cleavage and her very shapely derrière.

The last time I saw her was at the Cattle Barron's Ball, an annual charity event that raises funds for the American Cancer Society. Ann and I were in line to get our steaks when from across the way a well-tanned young lady in a very full white leather halter top and white leather shorts quickly approached us calling my name. I recognized her immediately. My client's ex-wife hugged me. I introduced her to Ann. She remarked to Ann, "I just love your husband." Ann had seen the ad in playboy and knew a little bit about the young lady. I was embarrassed. The couple who had gone with us to the party looked very amused. The husband told me that he would have loved for her to hug him too. He suggested that my status among the witnesses of the incident had risen considerably.

And Then There Were Masters

What started out as one of the most frustrating cases in my career turned out to be an extremely rewarding experience. It also resulted in a significant change in how temporary hearings for divorce cases are handled in Dallas, Houston, Fort Worth, Austin, San Antonio and El Paso.

In this case, I was representing a mother with four school-age children whose husband didn't come home from work one day. My client was a full-time mom who did not work outside the home. Mary had not received any support from her husband for about a month when we found the rat. Meanwhile, Mary and the children were living on donations from friends and from her church. Because of the over-crowded court dockets, I couldn't get a hearing set to provide temporary financial relief for almost four weeks.

For many years judges heard all of the temporary hearings in addition to final trials, motions to modify prior rulings, motions for contempt and everything else filed in their courts. It was not unusual to wait for a month to just get a hearing on the schedule. To get relief for their clients, some attorneys even resorted to stretching the truth a bit. They would request a Temporary Restraining Order or TRO that had to be heard within ten days. TROs were actually meant for emergency situations, but for some attorneys it seemed the best way to get their case heard in a timely manner. For the clients and the attorneys, the system really stunk. Somehow, Mary managed to feed her kids and pay her rent for four weeks, but as the date of her hearing neared, she was desperate for help.

Mary and I met two days before the hearing to prepare. Mary had created her financial information statement which detailed all of her recurring expenses. We reviewed the questions I would be asking her at the hearing and those she would probably be asked by her husband's attorney. We also discussed what she wanted to request of the Court. She wanted primary possession of the children and to have the use of the family home and her car during the pendency of the divorce. I told her how to get to the building that houses the family courts and asked her to meet me there at 9:00 the morning of the hearing. Our hearing was scheduled for 9:30.

On the day of the hearing, we met briefly in the hall and then took our place in the crowded courtroom. There were ten cases that day; all were set for 9:30. The judge started at the top of his list of scheduled cases calling the attorneys involved in each case to determine how much time they estimated their case would take. Our case was mid-way down the list. After going through the list, the judge told us to check back with him at 11:30.

As we left, I told Mary not to worry; that waiting to be heard was the rule, not the exception. We agreed to meet back at the court at 11:15. But when we went into the courtroom, the judge told us he wouldn't be able to hear our case until 1:30 that afternoon.

I was disappointed to be delayed again, and Mary, who was very apprehensive before the two delays, was now understandably upset. I took her to lunch at the cafeteria in the courthouse...and we waited. After what seemed to be an eternity, we returned to the courtroom at 1:30. The judge called the attorneys for our case to the bench and informed us that it would now be 3:30 that afternoon before he could hear our case.

I was not pleased at all with either the judge or the situation, but I never anticipated what would happen next. When we entered the courtroom at 3:30, a hearing was in progress. The judge called us back to the bench when the testifying witness finished. He explained that we would have to reschedule our case for another day because he was going to his son's baseball game that afternoon and would not have time to hear our case at all.

After telling him that I did not appreciate his failing to hear the case, I stormed out of the courtroom. Outside the courtroom I did all I could to reassure my hysterical client. Mary sobbed loudly as she asked how she and the children were going to live for the next month or so until the hearing could be rescheduled. I promised I would do everything I could to get a quick resetting. I cannot remember ever being as angry as I was that afternoon. I was so upset; I set my sights on finding a way to punish the judge for failing to hear our case.

Walking back to my office, I tried to figure out how to accomplish that goal. I called my wife to tell her I would be working late and went to the office law library to look up the statutes that created the courts in Texas.

When I was growing up, one of my mother's rules was: "You have no right to complain about something unless you have a proposed solution." In my quest for a way to get even with Judge Chrisman, I discovered a possible solution to the backlog of initial divorce hearings that often caused desperate clients like Mary to wait months or more to have their cases heard.

At about 8:30 that night, I ran across a statute

that applied only to Wichita County. The statute created a special master who had the authority to hear juvenile matters for the district court in Wichita County. I remembered participating in a hearing several months earlier that was conducted by a visiting judge from Wichita County. I had been very impressed with the visiting judge's knowledge and judicial temperament, so I looked up his home telephone number and called him.

After apologizing for calling him at home, I asked if he thought his master made a significant difference in how he handled the juvenile cases in his court. He said that his master worked a couple of days a week and took care of the juvenile matters in a very efficient manner, much faster than he was able to because of his regular docket. I asked if he thought that masters could handle temporary matters in divorce cases and, he said that he thought it would work really well. I thanked him for his time and promised to keep him up to date on my endeavor.

Now my anger was morphing into excitement as I began to imagine a solution to the huge problem facing the family courts where I spent all of my time. I knew the solution would require a state law, so I looked into the filing deadline for new legislation in the session in progress at that very moment.

I only had two weeks to draft a bill creating masters for Dallas County, get sponsors in the Texas House of Representatives and the Senate, get the support of the organized bar and convince the powerful people in Dallas County that masters could save the county money. I had to work quickly and, without the help and support of some very caring individuals, I would have had no chance to succeed.

Peggy Stewart, Judge Dan Gibbs' clerk, was the

most experienced administrator in the family court system. I went to see her the next morning to ask for statistics on the number of filings in the family courts, the number of temporary hearings, the cost of clerks, bailiffs, court reporters and, yes, even judges. Peggy was a tremendous help.

My next call was to a high school friend, Bill Melton. He was the administrative assistant to the very powerful Dallas county judge, the Honorable Lew Sterrett, who would later have a courthouse named after him. I asked Bill if he could set up a meeting with Judge Sterrett so I could pitch my idea to him from the perspective of saving money for the county.

Next, I called Richard Geiger, a member of the Texas House of Representatives. Dick and I worked in the same office building. We were friends, but not close. I asked if I could show him the legislation I had drafted with the hope of getting him to sponsor it in the House of Representatives. He agreed to sponsor the bill in the house and also offered to help me get a sponsor in the Senate. Luckily, Senator Oscar Mauzy agreed to sponsor the bill in the Texas Senate.

My project was gaining momentum. I met with Judge Sterrett and, with the use of the statistics from Peggy Stewart, was able to convince him that having masters would be much less expensive for the county than creating new courts. Each new court would require a clerk, a bailiff, a court reporter and a judge. A master would not need a clerk, a bailiff, or a court reporter, and the master would be paid substantially less than a judge. The county could fund three masters for the cost of one new court, and the family courts would be able to handle more cases with the masters.

Next, I wanted the support of the Dallas Bar

Association. I asked the bar director, who was the liaison to the Family Law Section, to present my proposed legislation to the Board of Directors. Unfortunately, the gentleman who was supposed to present the proposal over-imbibed the day of the meeting and did not present my proposal to the Bar Board of Directors. My legislation would have to stand or fall without the help of the organized bar.

Dick Geiger recommended that we get the proposed legislation on the "Consent Docket" of the Texas Legislature. If legislation affects only one county, you can get on the consent docket. For legislation on this docket to pass, you need support only from a majority of the representatives and senators from that county.

I scheduled a trip to Austin the next week to testify in support of the new legislation and arrived at the committee hearing armed with my statistics and copies of the proposed legislation. It was the first time I had ever testified before a house or senate committee. I was not apprehensive because I knew a number of the people I expected to be participating in the hearing.

The first person to question me in the hearing was pretty hostile to my proposal. (I later learned that his nickname was "mad dog.") After responding to several very nasty questions from him, I asked him if he realized that the legislation I proposed did not affect Harris County, which he represented. "Then why the hell am I here?" he said as he stormed out of the hearing room.

The Dallas County contingent approved the legislation (unanimously) by a voice vote and Dallas County was approved for masters. Unfortunately, after the legislation was approved one of the four sitting family court judges convinced another judge not to use masters for several years.

However, Judge Chrisman supported the program from its inception. He was and is a good and honorable man, but I'm really glad I got so angry at him. Helping create masters is probably my greatest contribution to how family law cases are handled in Dallas and other major metropolitan areas in Texas.

Although getting the legislation passed was time-consuming, I didn't neglect Mary. In that oft-postponed hearing, she was granted temporary support. And later I represented her in the divorce through which she received substantial child support.

I never told Judge Chrisman this story until recently. He had no memory of my being angry with him. He approved of my including the story in the book. He agreed that masters, now called associate judges, improved the way cases were handled by the family district courts.

WHAT WORKS AND WHAT DOES NOT WORK

When you have had an opportunity for over forty years to observe what destroys marriages, you can predict what works to make marriages last over an extended period of time. Divorce attorneys seldom get chances to help marriages survive. Marriages have to be tended, much like a vegetable garden. Without constant care, a vegetable garden will be overtaken by weeds and insects. Marriages need continual nurturing if they are to grow and develop. I have identified three factors which can help evaluate the health of a marriage.

1 COMMUNICATION

There has to be both verbal and emotional communication for a marriage to remain healthy. Over the years I have encountered many individuals who have believed that *talking at* the other party was communication. It takes two to have meaningful communication. Listening is probably more important than talking in communication between spouses. Interrupting your spouse while he or she is trying to express his or her feelings or opinion is almost always destined to stop any meaningful communication.

One example of how poor communication can threaten the life of a marriage occurred early in my practice. A lady called to make an appointment to see me about a divorce. When she arrived for her appointment, she was shown into my office. I like to start my initial interview by asking, "How can I help you today?" She explained that she was furious with her husband because of the way he had treated her on her birthday. He had given her a check for $12,000.00. To her, giving her a piece of paper represented an indifference to her needs and feelings. Irrespective of the large amount of the check, she would have far more appreciated a hug, an "I love you" and a quiet dinner at her favorite restaurant. I later learned that the husband did not think that anything was real if you could not see and touch it. To him, the check represented the kind of present which he would want most for his birthday. I realized quickly their different styles of communication were a real impediment to a healthy marriage. She was kinesthetic. Some psychologists have described it as a touchy, feely kind of communication. He was just the opposite. If he couldn't see it and read it, it wasn't real. I asked her if she would consider seeing a counselor who could help them understand the other's style of communication.

She reluctantly agreed to postpone filing for divorce and to see the counselor. To my great pleasure, I never filed a divorce for the wife. The counselor helped them understand how to communicate with each other. To my knowledge, they are still married.

Another example of poor communication occurred when I represented an actuary. In my experience, actuaries and accountants have about as much imagination and spontaneity as a watermelon. For him, everything had to be planned down to the minute. His wife loved spontaneous, unplanned dinners, trips and other activities. She was unhappy and filed for divorce. He wanted to try to save his marriage and agreed to follow any plan I suggested.

I had him buy a calendar for the next year and bring it to the office. We then set out to create what I called, "Planned Spontaneity." On a monthly basis, I scheduled conduct for him. January 15, "Send Flowers," January 21, "Take her to dinner," February 14, "Flowers and a surprise trip to Austin" and so forth throughout the year. The divorce was dismissed and for several years thereafter, I met with the actuary and created the calendar for the next year. Meeting the needs of the other person, whether with verbal or emotional communication is crucial to a healthy, happy marriage. Making declaratory statements has much greater chance of creating friction than asking questions. A good example would be to ask your spouse, "What could I do to make your day a better day?" However, the question, "Why do you always act like a total jerk?" is not the kind of question I am suggesting you ask. If you and your spouse are not communicating, your marriage is sick.

2 FINANCES

Over the years I have seen many marriages go on the rocks because of disputes about finances. Sometimes the problem is caused by the couple not having enough money to pay their bills. More often, the problem is that one spouse, typically the husband, does not want to share financial information with the other spouse. There exists an attitude that "I earned the money and I can do whatever I want and it is none of your business." Unless there is a pre-nuptial agreement which states to the contrary, all income earned or received during marriage in Texas is community property. There are times in almost every marriage when both parties need to contribute to the family's finances. Being willing to budget when times are tough is a necessity.

If your marriage has financial problems, your marriage is sick. If you also have communication problems, your marriage is critically ill.

3 PHYSICAL RELATIONSHIP

If the parties to the marriage have communication problems and financial problems, a lack of trust and respect is almost always created which is most often mutual. In all of my years of practice, there are only two cases I can remember where the physical relationship of the parties was not severely affected or destroyed when the parties lost respect and trust for each other. Who wants to be intimate with someone you no longer love, trust and respect and may not even like? The loss of the ability to communicate, both verbally and emotionally, contributes to the health of the marriage. If your marriage has all three of the problems discussed above, it is in the "intensive care ward" of the marital hospital. Decisive action is needed immediately or the marriage will surely die. It will take the full participation of the parties and a skilled therapist to try to put "Humpty Dumpty" together again.

It depresses me that by the time most clients get to me, their marriages are dead but there has been no funeral. I sometimes think my role is to be a funeral director who conducts tasteful, considerate services with the interests of the children put first whenever it is possible.

EVEN MORE CASES

The Empty Chair

The case was interesting for several reasons. The best family law judge at the court house at that time was Judge Annette Stewart. The other lawyers involved in the case were very capable. I represented the wife; Louise Raggio represented the husband; and Reba Rasor represented the husband's mother. The couple had one son. What made the case so unusual was that the husband's mother claimed that she owned all the property in the house of her son and daughter- in -law.

The husband's family was very wealthy, but he did not work regularly. The issues regarding the custody of the son were not difficult. The son was spoiled rotten by his mother, father and grandmother. Although efforts were made to resolve the matter without trial, it was difficult to agree to a resolution when the husband's mother asserted that she owned everything and there was no property to be divided between the husband and wife.

On the day the case was set for trial, everyone showed up except the husband. There were six chairs at the counsel table; one was empty. When the judge asked Mrs. Raggio where her client might be, she responded "My client has committed himself to the Terrell State Hospital for the insane." In fact, that is exactly what happened. The husband was frightened to death of his mother. He thought that if he crossed her or in any way disagreed with her she would leave him nothing in her will. He had voluntarily entered the mental hospital on a thirty-day commitment. The judge commented that she had never had that sort of thing happen before, but thought that she should grant a continuance so that the husband could appear and participate in the divorce.

The case was reset for about 45 days after the original setting in order to give the husband's attorney some time to prepare for trial after her client got out of the mental hospital. My client was frustrated with the fact that she was receiving little or no support from her husband while he was in the hospital. On the appointed day everyone showed up for trial except the husband. The judge asked Mrs. Raggio, "Where is your client?" With a somewhat sheepish look on her face Mrs. Raggio replied, "He's committed himself to Terrell again."

The judge announced that we were going to trial whether the husband was there or not. As a result of his failure to appear, once again there was an empty chair at the counsel table. Not having your client present for trial puts you in a very difficult situation. I proceeded to present my case on behalf of the wife. After I finished questioning my client she was cross examined by counsel for the husband and counsel for the intervening mother-in-law. I called the husband as my second witness. Of course I knew that he was not present and not available for testimony. I wanted to make sure that the appellate court knew that I had tried to have him testify. My situation was almost identical the one where Clint Eastwood talked to the empty chair during a political convention. Throughout the preceding I would make comments about how we could do various things had the husband showed up for trial. Needless to say, my client received exactly what she wanted with respect to all of the child-related issues.

The mother-in-law had undergone so many facelifts it looked like her skin might burst open any minute. She was taking the position that she had loaned everything in the house to her son and daughter-in-law and that nothing existed that was to be divided by the court. She acknowledged during cross-examination that many of the things in the house had been gifts. She asserted that all were conditional gifts based upon her son and daughter-in-law doing what she wanted. Since they failed to do so, she had the right to reclaim all of the furniture, pots, pans, rugs, cars, silver and china.

The judge ruled that all of the property in the house belonged to the husband and wife except for the specific things that the husband owned prior to marriage or that had been given to him during the marriage. The property was divided very favorably to my client and a very strange trial ended. Although my client worked, she was hoping that she would receive a large sum of money in the divorce. She wanted me to accept what she described as a solid gold lion's head necklace in lieu of paying her bill. I told her that I would consider it after the necklace was appraised. The appraiser told me that the necklace was gold plated and worth less than $500. In retrospect I should have taken it, because I never got paid. All I'll ever have from that case are the memories of the "empty chair."

The Disappearing Plaintiff

The call came from the Dean of University of Texas Southwestern Medical School in Dallas. I had previously gone to the medical school to lecture pediatric residents on aspects of the Texas Family Code that could affect decisions which needed to be made by the doctors and residents at the school.

The Dean was upset about a law suit which had been filed by a patient who had been treated in the emergency room of Parkland Hospital. He had sued everyone in the emergency room the night he was treated. Those sued included a medical student. The Medical School and Parkland had insurance for the doctors and residents, but not for the medical students who often worked at the hospital. The Dean explained that the medical students who worked in the emergency room wore badges which read "Dr. Jones," even though they were not yet doctors. The issue of medical students being sued while wearing badges which identified them as doctors was troublesome. That error was corrected soon after the suit was filed, but not in time to deal with the litigation involving the medical student.

I was inclined to assist the Dean, but the subject matter was outside my area of expertise. I responded that I would be willing to look into the matter to see if I could come up with any ideas. The investigation of the situation revealed some very interesting information. The patient was a young man from Iran. He had been in an automobile accident and had come to the Parkland emergency room for treatment. His complaints to the emergency staff, including the medical student, were that he had several cuts on his head and he suspected that his nose was broken. When he was informed that standard procedure in all automobile wreck cases included drawing blood to test for possible alcohol content, he ran from the emergency room, out of the hospital and into the night.

Several weeks later the lawsuit was filed with everyone in the emergency room being designated as defendants. One of the allegations in the suit was the failure to diagnose and treat a broken ankle. There were a number of witnesses who had seen the Plaintiff run from the emergency room when he was told that he would have his blood alcohol levels checked. I decided to try to find out more about the Plaintiff. My efforts revealed that the Plaintiff was in the United States on a student visa. I learned that he had been working as a waiter and had not attended school in over three years.

A quick call to a friend who did immigration law provided our foolproof course of action. The Immigration and Naturalization Service was notified about the non-student Plaintiff. Deportation proceedings were started immediately. With the Plaintiff back in Iran and therefore unavailable to participate in the case, the court dismissed the suit for want of prosecution. The Dean was most appreciative.

Sexual Discrimination in the Marine Corps

Success in the previous case led to a second interesting case involving the medical school. I received a call from the distraught father of a fifth-year neurosurgery resident. He informed me that his son had received orders to report to active duty in the

Marine Corps.

The young doctor was scheduled to complete the fifth year of his residency at the end of June. He had been a member of the Marine Corps reserves during his years in medical school and in the years of his residency. He had only two drills to attend to complete his military obligation. In April of that year he had worn a short-haired wig to his next-to-last drill. His wig was discovered during an inspection at that drill. He was told that if he wore the wig again, he would be called to active duty. I never understood why he wore the wig to the last drill, but he did. Once again it was discovered during inspection. Less than a month before he was to have completed his residency, he received a notice to report to active duty.

I was asked to keep him from being called to active duty so that he could begin his medical career after nine years of medical school and residency. There was no doubt that he had worn the wig after he had been told not to do so. How in the world could I present a persuasive case in support of his position? When you are at a loss for what to do, you need to read and think creatively. I obtained a copy of the Navy Regulations, which applied to Marines. After hours of frustrating reading of dry and boring regulations, I found a real gem. An obscure provision allowed women to wear short-hair wigs to drill. I decided to file a suit in Federal Court, alleging sexual discrimination against my male client and asking for a restraining order to prevent the Marine Corps from calling my client to active duty. I was not sure what to make of the fact that my case had been assigned to a Federal judge who was a retired Marine Corps colonel. The court had set a hearing to determine whether to grant the injunction against the Marine

Corps.

The legal officers for the Marine Corps scoffed at the suit. They let me know in no uncertain terms that my position had no merit whatsoever. I was polite to the major and colonel who represented the Corps. I had served in the United States Air Force and was respectful of military procedures and officers who outranked me. The Judge asked for the attorneys to come to his chambers prior to the start of the hearing. He asked me what I planned to do if the injunction was not granted. I informed him that I intended to hold a press conference regarding the case to inform the public of what I thought was a really foolish course of conduct on the part of the Marine Corps. He then informed the attorneys that he had read the pleadings of both sides. The Judge wanted to know if the Marine Corps would give my client credit for attending the last drill and terminate his obligation as a Marine Corps reservist. The response was an unconditional no. The judge, with a frown on his face, asked the lead Marine Corps attorney, "Don't you realize that Mr. Robertson has you by the short hair?" He suggested that the negative publicity to the Corps was not something he wanted to see. He ordered us to discuss the matter and return to his office. When we returned to his office, the Marine Corps attorney announced to the Court that they would give my client credit for the last two drills, withdraw the order to report to active duty and prepare papers showing that he had completed his obligations as a Marine reservist.

To this day, I have never heard of any other use of military regulations dealing with rights of female members of the military to allege sexual discrimination against a male member of our armed forces. My client and his father were very pleased with the outcome of the case, as was the Dean of the medical school.

"The Flat Bed Truck"

"There's a strange lady on the phone who wants to talk to you about a divorce," announced the receptionist. I answered the phone with my stock statement, "This is Charles Robertson; how can I help you?" She said, "Do you make house calls?" "I never have, but I might under the right circumstances," I responded.

She explained, "Honey, I am so fat that I can't get into my car anymore. I've got a big ole Cadillac Coupe DeVille with really big doors and I still can't get in even on the passenger side, let alone under the steering wheel. You may need to get a flat-bed truck and a hoist to get me up on the truck." I told her that I had a van with a lift for wheel chairs that might work. She told me that she had broken her last two wheel chairs, but that her new one could handle up to four hundred pounds. She commented that she just might break the lift on the van, but was willing to try. We were able to get her in the van and brought her to the office.

She wasn't kidding about being fat. She weighed over 350. It took three of us to push her up the wheel chair ramp. Being fat was not the only unusual thing about the lady. The diamond in her wedding ring was at least six carats. She had a Patek Philippe watch that must have cost twenty thousand dollars. She also had a great sense of humor. She was wearing a Mumu dress made of a beautiful silk fabric. I commented that I thought her dress was pretty and she responded, "I have all my clothes made overseas by Omar the tent maker." She volunteered, "My husband wants a divorce. He says he didn't marry a sow and he's not going to live with one."

I asked her if she wanted a divorce and she told me that she did not. I shared with her that I had been overweight as a child and it had really depressed me. "Do you want to lose weight?" I asked. "You bet your sweet ass I do" she responded. I made a proposal to her that I often make to overweight clients. I said, "I will give you a twenty dollar discount off of my fee for every pound you lose between today and the day you get divorced." She exclaimed, "Are you kidding me? I'll own your damn building. If you are not kidding me, hand me the phone!"

What happened next dumbfounded me. She called her doctor and told him to send a heavy duty ambulance to my office address. "He's been after me to check in to the hospital and have my jaw wired shut. And I'm going to do it." The ambulance came to the office and took her directly to Baylor Hospital near downtown Dallas. As she was being loaded into the ambulance she said, "Thanks a lot sweetheart, I won't be able to talk to you, but I'll have my doctor call you and let you know how I'm doing."

I never heard from the doctor. I called from time to time to see if she was still a patient. Almost eight months after our appointment, she called me. "You got to see me" she exclaimed gleefully. "I've lost 180 pounds and my husband says I'm HOT! I do not need a divorce so I guess you don't owe me any money after all." I learned later that she had inherited millions from her father who had been in the oil business. I saw in the obituaries about fifteen years later that her husband had died and was survived by his wife, who had almost been my client.

"Rolling on the River"

My client and a couple of his partners in a prestigious Dallas, law firm had decided to go on a fishing trip to Alaska. They had gone to catch salmon in one of the many rivers that flowed into the Pacific Ocean. After several days of successful fishing with guides, all of the guys except my client decided to try their luck offshore. My client, Jim, decided to fish one of the tributaries. His plan was to wade along the shore line and fish up the large stream which flowed into the river. He was having good luck that morning. He had caught and released several fish when he noticed an elderly man on the opposite bank who was fishing from the top of a large rock that protruded into the stream.

The old gentleman was using a hand-line which he tossed upstream and let float past the rock before he retrieved it for another cast. When the old fellow stood up to throw the line again, his foot slipped and he fell head first into the flowing stream. The man was being swept downstream toward the river. Jim dropped his rod and raced downstream along the bank, barely keeping up with the bobbing figure in the water. He knew that if he were to save the old fellow, he had to jump into the stream and swim toward him. Reaching a narrow point in the stream where it curved slightly, he dove into the water. It was frigid and moving swiftly. Jim was able to grab the jacket of the man and pull him onto the bank just past the curve. The old man had swallowed a lot of water. Jim rolled him onto his stomach, tilted his head to the side and pressed on his back. Water flowed out of his mouth and he started to cough and sputter. He was alive. When the old man sat upright, Jim could see that he was an Alaskan Indian.

He asked Jim if he would help him get back to his home. Jim readily agreed and asked the old fellow to sit there while he retrieved his rod and reel. The sun was shining, but the temperature was in the forties. Both men shivered as they walked along the bank for almost a mile before they came to a bridge which crossed the stream. Once across the bridge, they walked almost another mile north where they came upon a large building surrounded by smaller houses. "That is my home" the old fellow announced. Jim was confused. He knew about a large group of Indians who had a small town near the river, but the large building which the Indian had said was his home was a magnificent structure. As they approached the entrance, several younger Indians rushed toward them. "Father, Father, what has happened?" one of the younger men asked. After they were all inside the house, the old man explained how he had fallen into the stream and how Jim had saved his life.

The house had been filling up with adult men during the telling of the story of his rescue. Jim was being thanked by everyone in the room when the old man, who had regained his composure, asked, "Who are you and what do you do?" Jim responded, "My name is Jim Stevens. I came to Alaska to fish for salmon. I live in Dallas, Texas, where I am an attorney."

The old man stood and said, "I am Tall Bear, Chief of the Tlingit tribe. You will be rewarded for what you have done. Tell my son how we can contact you at your home." After a hearty meal with the Chief and his family and friends, Jim went back to the lodge where he was staying on the southern side of the stream. He felt really good about what he had done. Saving Tall Bear was better than catching salmon for sure. How much better would be the biggest surprise of Jim's life. That evening, Jim shared his story with his buddies who had been fishing in the ocean with poor results. Jim and his friends returned to Dallas the next day.

When Jim returned to work, he was curious about the tribe of Indians in Alaska. After several failures at spelling the name he had heard but not read, Jim stumbled onto information about the Tlingit tribe and its history. He discovered that in 1935 Congress had authorized the Tlingit tribe to file a claim for the loss of use and value of their native lands. Oil had been discovered on their ancestral lands, but had been taken away from the tribe on an earlier date by the government. The tribe had filed suit under the Alaska Native Claims Settlement Act. The case had been finally settled in 1968 for hundreds of millions of dollars. Tall Bear was the chief of a tribe which had untold wealth and resources.

Jim wondered how he might be rewarded. He thought he might get a nice box of salmon. But that was before a call came to him at work from an Indian who described himself as the business manager of the tribe. He asked a single question: "Would Jim's firm be interested in representing the Tlingit tribe in all legal matters?"

Without checking with the management committee or the senior partners, Jim responded, "It would be an honor to represent the tribe and Tall Bear." The tribe proved to be a great client for the firm and provided Jim a number of fishing adventures with Tall Bear over the years. Tall Bear provided the best example of why "one should not judge a book by its cover."

Tall Bear was a wise and proud man. He expected to be treated with respect. He planned a trip for his family to visit Hawaii. His wife, his sons and daughters and their spouses and children were all going on the trip. Reservations had been made for an entire floor of a famous hotel at Lahaina harbor in Maui. Tall Bear and his entourage traveled in their traditional Indian clothing. Upon arriving at the Pioneer Inn, the family representative went to the check-in counter. The manager was evidently not impressed with the way the people in the group were dressed. He told the representative that there had been a mistake and that no rooms were available.

When Tall Bear was informed, he instructed his son to find out who owned the Inn and where he could be located. Armed with the information that the owner's office was just two blocks away, Tall Bear and his son walked to the building. Tall Bear demanded to see the owner about a problem with the Inn. He was granted an audience with the owner. Tall Bear looked the man in the eye and announced, "I want to buy the Pioneer Inn." The owner replied, "It is not for sale." Tall Bear responded, "Everything is for sale, just write your price on a piece of paper and give it to me."

The owner wrote $3,000,000.00 on the piece of paper and handed it to Tall Bear. Tall Bear stated, "It is done. Give my son wiring instructions to your account. But before I wire the money, I want you to go with me to fire the manager who refused to give us our reserved rooms." The owner checked to see that Tall Bear really had the three million and then went to the Pioneer Inn and fired the manager. Jim told me that the family had a great vacation in their newly purchased property.

Several years later, I was representing Jim in his divorce. His wife had hired one of the best and toughest family lawyers in town. Jim was being generous and things were going reasonably well when I received a call from Jim with an unusual request. He told me that Tall Bear had called to tell him that the tribe no longer wanted to own the Pioneer Inn in Maui. Tall Bear had offered to sell the Inn to Jim for one million dollars. Jim wanted to buy the Inn, but he did not want it to be involved in the divorce proceeding. He wanted to know if he could acquire the Inn as his separate property while he was still married. I explained that it was possible, but that the papers would have to be constructed properly and we would have to get the consent of his soon to be ex-wife and her attorney.

I called the attorney and told him that Jim had always wanted to own a little inn and had the opportunity to acquire one if he moved quickly. I asked if his client would have any objection to the acquisition if there would be no community liability. I got a call back several days later that there would be no objection. In order to accomplish the goal of the Inn's being Jim's separate property, the contract, the note, the deed and any deed of trust needed to be written so that "Jim and his sole and separate property estate and not the community estate of Jim and his wife" would own and/or owe.

After the divorce, Jim and several partners paid Tall Bear's tribe for the Inn. It was sold several years later, making the partners a very good return. The Pioneer Inn is now owned by Best Western. And now you know the rest of the story.

WHAT I HAVE LEARNED IN 45 YEARS OF PRACTICE

People Are More Important Than Things!

1. **Only fools seek out confrontation.** My grandmother, who lived to be 102, told me that, "Only fools seek out confrontation." She explained that I would have enough confrontations in my career if I never sought out a single one. You are going to have enough fights and disagreements if you never seek out a single one.

2. **Do not represent observers; only represent participants.** If your client is not interested in helping, you should consider withdrawing from the case. A client who is working on his or her case and is intellectually curious is a real bonus.

3. **Fire any client** who tries to leverage a better property settlement with threats to seek custody of the children.

4. **Take time to thank good clients** for the opportunity to represent them.

5. **Consider litigation the last and worst option.**

6. **Thorough preparation increases the chance of settlement and reduces the likelihood of hearings and trials.**

7. **Treat the court staff and judges with courtesy and respect.**

8. Take advantage of the skilled mediators, arbitrators and helping professionals who are available.

9. Be knowledgeable of the law, rules and procedures used by the courts.

10. **Be willing to help deserving people** in need who may not be able to pay your usual fee.

11. **Participate in organized bar** association activities on a local, state and national level.

Remember that "Bread cast upon the water comes back ham sandwiches." No matter what you do in life, if you do it well and for a good reason, the reward will be greater than the cost of doing it. My grandmother taught me this lesson. She said that if I represented my clients well, they would send others to me for help. She said I should think of those who were referred to me by former clients as "Ham Sandwiches."

THE LAST CASE FOR NOW

The Unknown Heir

I had been practicing law for several years when my boss said he was going to ask the two probate judges to appoint me to represent the "unknown heirs" in probate cases. I had no idea what that meant or what it would entail. He explained that in cases in the probate courts, the judges would routinely appoint attorneys to make an inquiry as to whether or not all of the heirs of the decedent had been identified. Shortly thereafter, I received my first appointment. I did not realize until later in the process that I was expected to make a cursory inquiry and to report to the court that all of the heirs had been identified. I was as excited about finding one or more "unknown heirs" as a kid going on his first scavenger hunt. The facts of the case were as follows:

1. The decedent was a vice-president of a well- known national corporation;
2. The decedent had three children, one of whom had predeceased him;
3. The son who had predeceased him was believed to have had two children;
4. The other two children of the decedent were still alive; and
5. The decedent's wife had predeceased him.

The will left the estate to the decedent's three children in equal shares. The children of the son who had predeceased his father would inherit equal shares of what would have gone to their father. The task seemed fairly simple. I concentrated my efforts on learning about the son who had predeceased the decedent. Having grown up in a part of town where things were not always as they seemed, I wanted to talk to reliable witnesses who could give me information about the son. At the risk of sounding politically incorrect, I have always believed that the "staff members" in a wealthy home are the best sources of good information. I sought out the maid who had worked for the son. After a diligent search, I found her and asked, "Have you ever heard any rumors about any children who were born outside of the house?" "Children born inside the house" refers to children who are the legitimate children of the man and wife. "Children born outside of the house" are children fathered by the husband with someone other than his legal wife.

To my amazement and great surprise, she answered, "There was some talk about a baby girl being born outside of the house in El Paso." "About how long ago was that?" I asked. "It must have been ten years or more as best as I can remember" she answered. I thanked her and started to try and figure out how to establish the truth or falsity of the rumor.

I had no idea *how* to start my search, but I was sure *where* the search needed to start: El Paso, Texas. My efforts were not helped by the internet as they would be today, because it didn't exist. I decided to center my search on marriage, divorce and birth records in the El Paso area ten to twelve years before my appointment. I knew that the son had been married at the time of his death. His widow was reluctant to talk to me at first, but warmed up considerably when she learned that her children would be inheriting substantial property. She reported that she and her husband had been separated for several years about ten years earlier, but had reconciled about eight years before his death. She told me that they had never been divorced. That separation was the only thing she told me which helped with my investigation. Where had he lived during the separation?

I decided to call the American Consul in El Paso. I was pleased that the young man I talked to was just starting his career as was I. I asked for his help in solving what I thought was an interesting riddle. I asked if he could possibly search the divorce records in Ciudad Juarez for the two-year period during which the son of the decedent had been separated from his wife. He agreed to do so and get back with me after his search, explaining that he could not give the inquiry a high priority. I had been told that it was not uncommon for American couples to cross over into Mexico and get quick divorces. The Mexican authorities were not always very attentive to detail as long as the required fees had been paid. Could the son and some woman other than his wife, who represented herself to be his wife, have received a Mexican divorce?

Two to three weeks after my call, I received an excited call from the employee at the consulate. He had found the records of a Mexican divorce involving the son and his wife. I explained that the next step was to check the marriage records in El Paso to see if the son had married in the United States after the Mexican divorce. My helper was more enthusiastic about the task. His spirits had been buoyed by the success in finding the divorce records. He promised to review the records as soon as possible. Eureka! A marriage license had been issued in El Paso just two days after the Mexican divorce.

The next step in the investigative process was to search the birth records for the period following the issuance of the marriage license. I was hopeful that we would find the records of the birth of the child the maid described. Sure enough, just three weeks after the marriage license, a baby girl was born in El Paso and her birth certificate had the father and mother's names along with other helpful information. I now had two social security numbers which would help me later on. I also knew that Sheila was the name of my "unknown heir."

The plot thickens! Where was the little girl who would be twelve later that year? How could I find the child who might inherit hundreds of thousands of dollars? The Social Security office in Dallas was willing to help me locate the child's mother. After several weeks, I was told that the mother and child lived in Ironton, Missouri. I learned that Ironton, a small town of 1,400 residents, was the county seat of Iron County in the southeastern part of Missouri.

I called to talk to the mother of my "client." I was concerned about telling her too much about what might happen until I had some solid information. I learned that what I suspected had happened. She had been living with the son of the decedent and had gotten pregnant. She explained that they wanted to have the birth certificate show that the baby was born to parents who were married so that her daughter would not be considered illegitimate. I told her that she would probably have to bring her daughter to Dallas to appear in court. She complained that they did not have much money and wanted to be assured that it was absolutely necessary that they come to Dallas.

For the two month period before I found Sheila, the attorneys who represented the two surviving children and the two children of the son who predeceased his father had been calling and writing about the status of my investigation. Two of the best probate lawyers in Dallas were involved in the case. One represented the two surviving children and the other represented the two children of the deceased son. To say that they were growing irritated with me was an understatement. Little did they know that they would soon become even more irritated. One or both of them had complained to the judge who had appointed me about the delays. The court coordinator had called me to ask why I had not filed my report with the court. She intimated that the judge was not pleased with my lack of action.

I had never filed a report with the court regarding the results of trying to locate unknown heirs because this was the first time I had ever been appointed. My report was short and to the point. I stated that I had found a previously unknown heir. I listed her name and address in my report. Over the next several weeks, the attorneys for the other parties both filed pleadings with the court alleging that Sheila was illegitimate and had no right to inherit under Texas law. The attorneys thought that they had an ironclad defense against Sheila receiving anything. They asserted that her father was married to someone other than Sheila's mother. I think that they expected to roll over me like Sherman in Georgia. I was young and inexperienced but armed with knowledge they never anticipated. I had studied family law under one of the true experts in Texas. I had been taught that if the parties, Sheila's mother and father, had attempted to marry, even if there was a legal impediment to the marriage, the offspring of that union would not be illegitimate. I filed a responsive pleading and a brief citing the case law which supported my position.

229

I filed an additional pleading asking the court to rule that Sheila was the only heir entitled to inherit anything from her grandfather. When the judge and the other two attorneys saw that pleading, all hell broke loose. I know that the next part of this story will be dull and boring, but it is crucial to what happened. The will of the decedent contained an "In terrorem clause." An In terrorem clause is defined in Black's Law Dictionary as follows:

"A condition 'in terrorem' is a provision in a will which threatens beneficiaries with forfeiture of their legacies and bequests should they contest the validity or dispositions of a will."

I argued in my pleading that Sheila was legitimate and that the other beneficiaries had contested dispositions under the will, which would give her the right to receive one-ninth of the net estate of her grandfather. If the judge ruled in Shelia's favor, as the law required, she would have received millions, not hundreds of thousands of dollars. I was told by the coordinator to be in court the next morning at nine o'clock. With a large amount of fear and trepidation, I went to the probate court the next day. If you have never been screamed at by two lawyers and one judge at the same time, let me tell you it is not pleasant. After the group scream subsided, they would alternate delivering unkind remarks about me.

The judge asked why I was trying to insult the court and two of the best probate attorneys in Dallas. "I am just trying to do what I was appointed to do: represent the unknown heirs," I answered. "If the two attorneys have filed pleadings which might get them in trouble with their clients, why don't you let them withdraw their pleadings and acknowledge my client's rights?" I queried. One of the attorneys commented, "Judge that might just solve a lot of problems."

The Judge, still full of rage, glowered at me and stated, "I will let them withdraw their pleadings and you will never be appointed to anything else by this court."

Fortunately for Sheila, before the case concluded, it was transferred to another court to equalize the number of cases in each court. I had the opportunity to talk to Sheila on the phone several times before there were any court proceedings. The new judge and I had been college classmates. He knew me and trusted me. As I expected, it was necessary for Sheila and her mother to come to Dallas for a hearing which concluded the probate of her grandfather's estate. The judge told Sheila that she was a lucky young lady to have had someone looking out for her interests.

During a break, Sheila asked if we could talk alone. Her mother did not object, so Sheila and I sat down on one of the long benches outside of the courtroom to talk. What Sheila said really shocked me. "Mr. Robertson, I don't trust my mother to take care of my money. Would you look after it for me?" "What do you think she would do?" I asked. Sheila looked very sad and responded, "I think she would spend it all." At that time in Texas, children did not reach majority until age twenty-one. Money had to be held in trust for their benefit and spent only with court permission. I asked if she would tell the judge what she had told me if her mother was not present. She nodded affirmatively.

Sheila and I went into the judge's chambers. The judge asked Sheila what she would like to talk about. Gently sobbing, she explained that she did not trust her mother and wanted me to take care of her money. The judge smiled and said, "Mr. Robertson and I will both take care of your money for you." I was appointed to be the trustee of Sheila's money. By the time all of the expenses of the estate were paid, Sheila's share was in excess of two hundred and forty thousand dollars. I suggested to the judge that I be allowed to buy two jumbo CD's. Each Certificate of Deposit cost $100,000.00. He agreed and I went shopping. I bought nine year certificates which would mature after Sheila had reached twenty-one. I was able to get 17.5% interest. The judge and I agreed to put $10,000.00 into a money market account earning 10%. We hoped that Sheila could operate on the forty thousand plus interest until she received the rest of the money after her twenty first birth day. If you don't know about the "Rule of 72," I am going to teach you now. You can divide 72 by the interest rate you are receiving and it will tell you how long it will take to double your money. For example, 72 divided by .175 equals 4.11. Sheila's money would double every 4.11 years. Sheila's $200,000.00 would be worth $800,000.00 by her twenty first birth day. The judge and I agreed that having $800,000.00 when you were twenty-one would give you one heck of a start toward building an estate.

I wanted to give Sheila an allowance, but the judge was not sure that was a good idea. I won that argument and Sheila received a small monthly amount. We talked on the phone from time to time about how she was doing in school. When she turned sixteen, she called me to ask if there was any chance she might be able to have a car. She had passed the written and driving exams and had her driver's license. I approached the judge with the idea of buying Sheila a car. He told me that neither of his children had cars at 16 and he didn't think Sheila needed one either. After several discussions, the judge relented and allowed me to buy a used Honda Civic for Sheila. She was thrilled with her car. She was a very responsible young lady who did very well in school. We had a discussion during the fall of her senior year about where she wanted to go to college. She wanted to go to a small state college not too far from Ironton. The judge was much easier to convince that spending money on tuition, books, room and board was an appropriate use of her money market funds. We never had to cash in either of the original CD's. Interest rates had fallen significantly after President Carter's term was over. I used to get calls from the bank on a regular basis asking me if I didn't want to cash out of the CD's. By the time Sheila turned twenty-one, the rates were back into the high single digits.

After the end of her sophomore year, Sheila called to tell me that she was engaged. Her boyfriend had graduated and was starting to work. She planned to finish college. She was almost twenty by the time school started for her junior year. In the spring semester of her junior year, she called to ask if there was any chance that the judge might let her have enough money to make a down payment on a small house. She and her fiancé had decided to get married the summer before her senior year. I approached the judge with her request. He was not enthusiastic at all. He said he would not even consider it unless Sheila and her fiancé came to Dallas to talk to him in person. I reminded him that she would be twenty-one in November and would be entitled to all of her money.

Sheila and her fiancé came to Dallas to meet the judge. He spent over an hour with them in his chambers. He and I talked after their visit. He said, "They are both really good kids. Let's give them the down payment for the house—but not until they agree to meet with a good financial advisor about what to do with Sheila's money."

After Sheila's twenty- first birthday, she received a check of over $800,000.00. That first Judge never appointed me to represent the unknown heirs in his court again. The one time I was appointed and what happened thereafter represents one of my favorite experiences as an attorney.

APPENDIX

Contributions to the Profession

I hesitated to write this chapter. There is a great chance that you will think that I am just "tooting my own horn." The reason for including my activities with the organized bar and related organizations is to try to convince you to get involved, whatever your profession or avocation. Be a participant, not an observer. You always get more out of doing good work than you have put into it.

1. **FORMS FOR DIVORCE AND ANNULMENT.** In 1969, Title One of the Texas Family Code, "Husband and Wife," passed the legislature to become effective on January 1, 1970. As discussed in the chapter titled "The Last Semester," I created forms which became the first form book ever published by the State Bar of Texas.

2. **CHAIRMAN OF THE FAMILY LAW SECTION DALLAS BAR ASSOCIATION, 1973-74.** From the first day I went on active duty with the United States Air Force, it had been drilled in to me, "Never volunteer for anything." But my time in the service had given me a very contrary experience. I had learned that if you volunteered to do the worst or hardest job and did it well, you could leap-frog others vying for leadership positions. I decided that I would join the Dallas Bar Association in addition to the State Bar of Texas and the American Bar Association. I wanted to become the chairman of the Family Law Section of the Dallas Bar Association. It usually took twelve to fifteen years of devoted service in a section of the Dallas Bar to rise to the top

position. Long before personal computers or facile communication had been created by the internet and email, the worst job in the Family Law Section was treasurer. You had to hustle to collect dues and recruit new members of the section. After being a member of the section two years, I had learned that no one wanted the job and my volunteering to take on the burden was well received. The ladder to the chairmanship of the section went from treasurer to secretary to vice-chairman to chairman-elect to chairman. I became the treasurer for the 1972-1973 year. The secretary of the section had held that position for several years and did not aspire to a higher position. A very fortuitous series of events occurred which elevated me to the chairmanship of the Family Law Section for 1973-1974. The vice-president moved out of the Dallas area to help take care of his elderly parents and the chairman-elect was appointed by the governor to be the judge of a criminal district court.

Being the chairman of the section, along with my work on the form book, led to an unexpected reward which I treasure to this day.

3. FAMILY LAW COUNCIL.

The Family Law Section of the State Bar of Texas has a group of members who meet regularly to direct the section's activities. The Family Law Council is made up of attorneys, judges and professors who have a special interest in family law. I was honored by being invited to be a member of the Council in mid 1970s and served on the Council for several years. We worked to improve the law and to make materials available to lawyers in Texas. The Family

Law Practice Manual was the successor to the original form book I created and is still used today. It has been updated every few years and is available now in printed form as well as on disc for computers. Most of the really skilled family lawyers in Texas have served on the council over the years I have been practicing.

4. CHAIRMAN OF THE FAMILY LAW EXAM COMMISSION.

In 1974 the State Bar of Texas created the Texas Board of Legal Specialization. Richard West was the director. Attorneys could take a six-hour exam in a specific area of the law and be certified as a specialist in that area if they passed the examination, had practiced for at least five years, and devoted a required percentage of their time to that area of practice. I beat the deadline for practice by several weeks and signed up to take the exam. The State Bar conducted a course in Houston to get candidates ready to take the family law exam. I was a bit miffed that I was not asked to participate in the seminar as a speaker. For reasons I still do not understand, the drafter of the exam was also not invited to be on the faculty of the course. It is my understanding that he was more than a bit miffed.

I decided that I would not attend the prep course. With Allen Morris, a family lawyer, friend and captain of my softball team in the Dallas Junior Bar league, I decided to drive to Austin to take the exam. The plan was for him to drive to Waco, which is exactly half way to Austin, while I quizzed him about family law and for me to drive from Waco to Austin while he quizzed me. As we were pulling into the parking area of the motel where we were staying, Allen announced that he thought we didn't need to study anymore and that we should relax by the pool and have a few margaritas.

The exam was tiring, but not difficult. We drove back to Dallas feeling really good about our chances. About six weeks later, I got a call from the Texas Board of Legal Specialization in Austin. The caller was very upset about the results of the family law exam. The grader, who was also the drafter, had failed seventy percent of the people who took the exam. The Board of Specialization was worried that if the word got out about the failure rate, no one would sign up to take the exam in the future. I asked why I was being called. The caller explained that I had done very well on the exam and the Board wanted me to re-grade the exams. I promised to think about it and call him the next day.

I thought about how the process should work and proposed that if the Board would make me the chairman of the "Family Law Examination Commission" and let me appoint three other attorneys who would write the exam and grade it, I would agree. The Board agreed and consented to my other conditions. The attorneys I asked to participate on the commission were drafters of portions of the Texas Family Code and experts in family law. The model which we put in place was adopted by the other areas of specialization.

The bar would pay our expenses each year to come to Austin to draft the exam and to return to Austin to grade the exam after it had been administered to the candidates. The plan was to arrive on Thursday afternoon and talk about how the exam needed to be changed. I would assign questions to be written by the commission members, who would also write the answer to the question.

On Friday morning we would take turns presenting the questions we had written and defending our answer to the other members. We decided to change one-third of the exam each year. New rules, Texas Supreme Court decisions, new laws and Court of Appeals decisions were the source of material for new questions. I served as the chairman for about eight years.

5. **DRAFTED LEGISLATION WHICH CREATED COURT MASTERS FOR FAMILY DISTRICT COURTS IN TEXAS.** See the chapter, "And Then There Were Masters."

6. **CHAIRMAN OF THE DALLAS BAR ASSOCIATION'S JUDICIARY COMMITTEE** which published the first BENCH BOOK for Dallas County in 1992.

7. **CO-AUTHOR OF THE TEXAS FAMILY LAW TRIAL GUIDE**
The Trial Guide functioned almost like a "manual computer" in that it allowed the user to quickly find the answer to almost any family law question. Jo Lynne Merrill and Bill Dorsaneo worked with me on the concept for the book which was published by Matthew-Bender. Until computer research became widely available and used, the Trial Guide was the best research tool.

8. CREATED THE MENTAL HEALTH DIRECTORY FOR NORTH TEXAS

I was appointed to represent a six year old girl who had been sexually abused. She could not speak English. It took me about a month to locate Delores Vela, a trained counselor who was fluent in Spanish. I decided that there was a real need for a directory of psychologists, psychiatrists, licensed professional counselors and other experts who could help children with educational and emotional problems, including adjusting to divorce. The first directory was published in 1975 and a new edition was published every five years until 1995 when the family law section started publishing a manual which duplicated what I had been doing. I distributed copies to the courts, family law section members, all of the people in the directory, school counselors, preachers, priests and rabbis.

9. FOUNDING MEMBER OF THE LEGAL ASSISTANTS DIVISION OF THE STATE BAR OF TEXAS.

I felt that there should be recognition for the non-lawyers whose talent and ability did a great deal to help their attorneys to deliver quality work for their clients.

10. DRAFTED AND GRADED THE FIRST LEGAL ASSISTANT FAMILY LAW SPECIALIZATION EXAMINATION.

Special status and recognition should be available to those whose knowledge and ability sets them apart from other legal assistants.

11. PROPOSED AND PLANNED THE FIRST BENCH BAR CONFERENCE OF DALLAS BAR.

While chairman of the Judiciary Committee of the bar, I helped create a conference where the judges and attorneys who practiced in their courts could engage in a dialog about how to improve the legal system. Getting to know the judges in a setting outside of the courtroom greatly improved communication and cooperation of all involved.

12. MEMBER OF THE AMERICAN ACADEMY OF MATRIMONIAL LAWYERS.

The AAML is a national group of family lawyers who are dedicated to improving the process for people involved in domestic matters and to elevating the standards of attorneys who practice family law. It was an honor to be asked to join and is a pleasure to know many of the best family lawyers in the United States.

53049615R00140

Made in the USA
Lexington, KY
24 September 2019